THE STRANGE STORY OF THE GOSPELS

After National Service in Germany from 1947 to 1949, Leslie Houlden studied History and Theology at The Queen's College, Oxford. He was ordained in 1955 to a curacy at Hunslet, South Leeds. He taught at Chichester Theological College and was then Chaplain Fellow of Trinity College, Oxford from 1960 to 1970. He was Principal of Cuddesdon Theological College and Vicar of Cuddesdon from 1970 to 1977. At King's College, London, 1977–1994, he was a New Testament lecturer, then Professor of Theology. He is the author of numerous books on the New Testament and Christian theology.

In gratitude to
the Master and the Community of the
Foundation of Lady Katherine Leveson
at Temple Balsall

The Strange Story of the Gospels

Finding Doctrine through Narrative

Leslie Houlden

Published in Great Britain in 2002 by
Society for Promoting Christian Knowledge
Holy Trinity Church
Marylebone Road
London NW1 4DU

British Library Cataloguing-in-Publication Data

A catalogue record for this book is available from the British Library

ISBN 0-281-05436-3

Typeset by Trinity Typing, Wark on Tweed
Printed in Great Britain by
Antony Rowe Ltd., Chippenham, Wiltshire

Contents

Acknowledgements

Bible quotations are from the Revised Standard Version of the Bible, copyright 1946, 1952 and 1971 by the Division of Christian Education of the National Council of the Churches of Christ in the USA. Used by permission. All rights reserved.

The publishers acknowledge with thanks permission to reproduce extracts from the following:

W. H. Auden, 'In Memory of W. B. Yeats', from *Collected Poems*, Faber & Faber.

Extract from 'A Church in Bavaria', from *Collected Poems* by William Plomer published by Jonathan Cape. Used by permission of The Random House Group Limited.

R. S. Thomas, 'The Kingdom', from *Collected Poems, 1945–1990*, J. M. Dent.

Introduction

Every word of the title carries weight. There is also ambiguity. For example, to speak of 'the Gospels' is to refer to the collection seen as a single entity. But it may also point to each of the four once-independent writings that make up the collection: it could be that each of them is screaming for release from the straitjacket imposed since the second century by being bound up with the others. So we can think of either the group or the items that make it up. The 'story' may refer to the tale of Jesus' origins, ministry, death and resurrection which all of the Gospels tell, each in its own special way (so that the singular 'story' conceals the plural 'stories'). But it can also refer to the story of the books themselves: how they began, how they have fared down the centuries, especially in the use given by the Church, and again each is distinct. And 'strange' is an adjective worth trying on either of those senses of 'story'. The story of Jesus is full of strangeness, whether as told in the Gospels or when we look at it as an episode of history or when we consider its extraordinary effects. But the career of the Gospels as distinct books is also full of surprising turns, enough to madden the evangelists if we can suppose them to have natural human reactions to their beloved and momentous works. The twists and turns of that career (or four distinct careers) are little attended to, whether in scholarly books on the Gospels or among hearers of the Gospels in snippets in church services or indeed among their devout readers. Ambiguities can annoy; these ambiguities are intended to fascinate, even to improve life for the liturgical hearers and devout domestic readers. Fascination can be a road to sanctity.

Until fairly recently, the Gospels operated almost wholly within the Church: in that sense, we may say that the Church 'owned' them. They have occupied a role in 'Christian teaching'. Some people wish (or behave as if) they had never found their way anywhere else. But for getting on for three centuries, and with increasing vigour, they have found a home in the academy, itself increasingly vigorous in its independence of the Church and often at variance with its devout or sluggish ways. That interest has been historical and, in a variety of ways, literary or linguistic: what did these texts originally 'say' to their readers, whence did they derive, how are they structured? They have also escaped (sometimes not very sensibly – or is that just church or academic prejudice?) into the secular literary world: they are books worth attending to, whatever you think or do not think about Jesus. In these ways, there has been no confining these books in a single environment. If there is a question of their being 'abused' in the process, then we shall see that they are no strangers to abuse – on every hand.

This book is not about 'the Jesus of history'. That subject has had ample exposure for many years, with a huge spurt of academic activity over the recent Millennium. The Gospels stand between us and Jesus, operating as screens, windows or walls. It is not the concern of this book to decide where or how far each of those images is appropriate; though there is no denial here that the Gospels are the major illumination of Jesus that is available to us (though that idea too is not without ambiguity). No, the subject is the Gospels and their strange story.

We begin with a chapter that takes up what has been outlined in this introduction and delves more deeply. Then there are chapters exploring each of the Gospels in the light of it. Finally, there is an attempt to view the whole matter in the light of Christian theology as an enterprise. Readers of earlier books will see it as another (but I hope different) attempt to sing a familiar song. I think it is still worth singing, perhaps more than before; and the Gospels encourage it, for they were its first singers.

The book began as a series of autumn lectures given at St Giles in the Fields in London in the year 2000. I am grateful to the Rector (and Archdeacon of Charing Cross), Dr W. M. Jacob, for inviting me to give them and to him and the friendly audience for constant encouragement. They had a partial second outing at Norwich Cathedral a few months later, in equally happy circumstances, thanks to the Dean, Stephen Platten, and to Fr Douglas Brown. Another old friend, Ruth McCurry of SPCK, seized the chance of urging a book. One can only comply.

1

The Gospels and the Doctrine: A Cloudy Relationship

On the day called Sunday there is a meeting in one place of those who live in cities or the country, and the memoirs of the apostles or the writings of the prophets are read as long as time permits.

(Justin, *First Apology*, Chapter 67)

This chapter has three parts. First, some elementary information about the Gospels, by way of orientation. Then, a similar introductory treatment of Christian doctrine, as it has emerged and is customarily presented. Finally, discussion of the relation between the two, chiefly as it has been over the centuries. At this point, the strangeness referred to in the Introduction comes into view.

THE GOSPELS

Much about the origins of the Gospels remains unsure, as might be expected. They were written within a small and, at the time, obscure movement, and by the time they came more into the open, only legends about their beginnings were available. Nevertheless, we have the books, and many questions that arise can be answered with sufficient assurance. Here, those answers will be treated as if they were facts. For the purposes of this book, readers will not go seriously astray.

Dates are good for orientation, all that follow being from the first century AD:

30	End of Jesus' ministry.
35	Paul converted to share in the Christian mission.
40–60	Paul's main mission work among gentiles; and letter-writing.

mid-60s	Death of Paul.
66–74	Jewish revolt against the Romans in the Holy Land.
70	Jerusalem shattered, temple destroyed; church in Jerusalem dispersed, so end of visible centre for the Christian movement. Unclear whether strongly felt, but in principle a major moment.
70	Whether by coincidence or not, the writing of first Gospel – that of Mark. That is, at this point, someone decided to take this step: writing out the faith by way of the story. Worth asking: did it 'need' to happen? What if it had not, ever? Might the Church have subsisted on Paul alone? (See Chapter 2.)
85–90	Successors undertake comparable task: Gospels of Matthew and Luke, using Mark as basis. (See Chapters 3 and 4.)
90–100	More independently, the writing of the Gospel of John. (See Chapter 5.) And the less comparable Gospel of Thomas, with only sayings of Jesus, i.e. no story-line, failed to commend itself to the Church in general.

What are the Gospels?

The answer seems obvious: they are accounts of the origins, life, teaching, death and resurrection of Jesus of Nazareth. In various ways they are, as we might expect, not unlike 'lives' of great men written in this period; though the genre is diverse (see Burridge, 1992). Moreover, those lives mostly come from the small literary top layer of Greco-Roman society. The Gospels come from much lower down the social scale; and they survived only within the relatively small (though effective) Christian network. (Within a few years, copies of these books had found their way, from places of origin in (let us suppose) Asia Minor, to Egypt, where they survived in fragmentary form until the papyrus discoveries in modern times.)

We can improve upon the obvious answer. Let us define the Gospels as the Christian faith put in narrative form. That is to say, whatever their literary shape, their aim is not biographical in the usual modern sense. They do not tell the tale of the life simply for the sake of the story (though this is not to deny that modern biographies quite often have an axe to grind). The aim of the Gospels is then perfectly expressed by the ending of the main body of the Gospel of John: 'these [things] are written that you may believe that Jesus is the Messiah, the Son of God, and that believing you may have life in his name' (John 20.31). They were not written for entertainment or for educational reasons, but with theological intent and for an evangelistic purpose.

The question of their purpose can be answered in another way. What were they written for? Almost certainly for reading aloud in church meetings, and surely in a liturgical setting; though, to avoid a modernizing impression, it is wise to say a quasi-liturgical setting. As we shall see later, they may have been written to be read in sections or as wholes. If in sections, then we should beware of imagining those sections were as brief as in modern liturgies, where the exposure is transient in the extreme. As to reading aloud: the practice remains in the orthodox rabbinic seminary, but elsewhere (except in liturgical brevity) is found inconvenient – despite its aesthetic and formative qualities. But to grasp the Gospels' beginnings, it is worth always having in mind Augustine's story of Ambrose of Milan (*Confessions*, Book 6), where the bishop is spied reading: his lips move but no sound emerges – and it is noteworthy. A few earlier (aristocratic) examples have been adduced, but, for our purpose, this instance from the 380s will serve. 'Reading' meant reading aloud; and, for almost everybody, to encounter a book meant to hear it read.

Correlative to 'reading' as, for most, a form of listening is the centrality of rhetoric in education; that is to say, the art of persuasive speech. Children learnt the means to convince by the framing of argument and the decoration of speech. Its correlative is the art of listening and learning, by recognizing patterns of recurring words and of reasoning and allusions to familiar authoritative texts. Apart from those engaged in advocacy and politics, it is of course a lost art. So it is not surprising that its functioning is lost on modern readers (in their silence and privacy), and the working of its techniques strikes us as peculiar: why, for example, all those allusions to Old Testament episodes and texts, and why two almost identical miracles of feeding in the

Gospel of Mark? Well, so that, with luck, the reader might notice and seize the point being conveyed. No chance, after all, of going back and reading again; so the mark must be made here and now. Later, we shall find connections between passages being made that seem far-fetched. The explanatory context is the first-century mode of reading and hearing.

Who wrote the Gospels?

We turn to a more down-to-earth question, on a par with the matter of dates. It helps the tidy mind to face the matter of authorship even if only to lay it aside as either relatively unimportant or unanswerable. Internally, all the Gospels are anonymous, and, as far as evidence goes, the attributions of authors' names belong to the first half of the second century, at least as far as Matthew and Mark are concerned. The suspicious modern mind notes the tendency in that period to consolidate the Christian resources on apostolic foundations wherever possible: good authority was a major benefit. Hence Papias of Hierapolis (early second century, quoted by Eusebius two centuries later) sees Mark as indeed the author of the book ascribed to him and as the recorder of Peter's memories. But his credibility is not enhanced by his ignoring of the plain (and long-seen) relationship between Mark and Matthew. And we are bound to note the importance of apostolic unity and authority visible in the very formation of and the arrangement of the books within the Christian canon, the New Testament – a process that may well go back to this very period, the mid-second century. Indeed, the later books of the canon itself (e.g. the Pastoral Epistles ascribed to Paul, and Acts) are already moved by the quest to find peace and unity in the context of a cohesive Church grounded in the apostles. The process is no doubt aided by the loss in AD 70 of a visible geographical centre for the Church that was referred to earlier (see Trobisch, 2000). But the cases may vary: Luke's name (though not absent, and usefully Pauline in its associations, 2 Tim. 4.11) is not central to early Christian affairs, and that speaks for authenticity. The links with 'John' (but which?), while probably indirect, have claims to be genuine; however, they are likely to be venerable but for many purposes tenuous (see Hengel, 1989).

But these discussions dwindle in importance, for we know so little of the people concerned, and it is evidently a matter to be viewed within the context of wider early Christian development and the forces by which it was affected: the need for cohesion and authenticity of faith in the midst of tendencies to fall apart in belief and structures. The upshot is that, if our concern is with them in themselves, we must see the Gospels as books standing on their own pairs of feet, while no doubt flowing from a variegated process of tradition concerning Jesus in the years before they were written.

CHRISTIAN DOCTRINE

This section is briefer, its main point being simply to indicate a different kind of factor in Christian life from that which we find in the Gospels. As with them, there should be an attempt at definition. Christian doctrine is the statement of Christian faith and devotion in words and ideas, with the purpose of teaching, whether within or outside the Church. So it may express itself in various kinds of brief formulas or much longer and more elaborate treatises, or indeed full systematic treatments of Christian teaching in whole or in parts. Especially in such ampler expressions, there will usually be a philosophical undergirding of one kind or another. In turning to doctrine, therefore, we have moved from 'story' to 'concept'.

In terms of this broad definition, it is evident that Christian writing (and perhaps a great deal of typically Christian talk?) began as 'doctrine'. The demarcation between 'story' and 'doctrine' is of course not absolute, especially in our case; for the story of Jesus, in one form or another, is basic to Christian understanding. But if we think of a formula like that found in 1 Corinthians 15.3–5 (or 7), or of the 'hymn' in Philippians 2.5–11, while there is a narrative and historical aspect, we do not err to see the purpose as doctrinal: they are attempts to put faith in terms of ideas.

Such attempts are likely to focus on the following:

- God as the fount of all;
- Jesus as his agent for salvation;
- Jesus' coming, death, resurrection, and triumph including his return and his ultimacy – for ever.

One aspect or another may be taken for granted, e.g. the first makes no appearance in the brief statements referred to above. Such statements of teaching may serve perhaps surprising purposes: that in 1 Corinthians 15 validates Paul's mission; that in Philippians 2 serves to urge us to be humble. But we can see that, in themselves, these formulas are doctrinal in character. They are vehicles of the faith.

In the sense of the discussion so far, we can say that Paul's letters (written before any of the Gospels) are full of doctrine, statements of important aspects of Christian belief put in 'thought' terms of one sort or another. And, as is well known, apart from the narrative of the Last Supper in 1 Corinthians 11.23–25 and two clear statements of Jesus' teaching (1 Cor. 7.10 and 9.14, to neither of which he gives unqualified assent), he tells us nothing about Jesus' life between his birth (Gal. 4.4) and his death, and both are seen chiefly in 'doctrine' rather than 'story' terms. (True, there are several other possible allusions to sayings of Jesus, but they are not clearly attributed and critics tend to be maximizers or minimizers. And what has been said should not make us think that Paul was 'cold' or 'abstract' in his response to Jesus, as a statement like that in Gal. 2.20 makes plain.) On the other hand, if Paul is, in our present terms, more 'doctrine' than 'story', the Gospels are, as we shall see, 'doctrine-by-way-of-story': but that takes us too far too quickly.

As Christian doctrine (belief expressed in one or another form of reasonable discourse) developed, it maintained essentially the scheme and content that have been stated: God as fount of all; Jesus as his fully authorized agent whose death and exaltation lead us to our salvation. Of course the scheme became more elaborate and more precise, for example by attending to the Spirit, drawing attention to God's present activity in Church and world; but the principles remained. In the developing creeds, emerging in due course as the Apostles' and the Nicene Creeds of familiar church use, the pattern of doctrine endures. It is found too in liturgy, for example in the eucharistic prayer of the *Apostolic Tradition* of Hippolytus, where the matter of the baptismal (effectively, the later Apostles') creed is closely paralleled. We are to worship God according to the pattern of faith, in which we are both baptized and subsequently live. Catechisms too, as they develop, while ranging more widely and with practical intent (dealing, for example, with the Lord's Prayer as the pattern for Christian prayer) show a similar agenda.

We must then notice that this pattern omits all reference to the greater part of the content of the Gospels! It is a symptom that had a big future. But could it not be justified? After all, in summaries, one goes for what is essential, that is, arguably the points laid out above, concerning God and Christ. One cannot always say everything, so one selects what really matters. But it is hard to deny that the policy leaves the Gospels beached – or, to make the point less dramatically, leaves them, despite their overriding aim of 'preaching the good news', going along a very different path, marked by Jesus' deeds and teachings. One could understand a plaint of evangelists: why did we bother?

STRAINED RELATIONS

The relations of our two modes of Christian expression, represented in the New Testament by the Gospels in the one case and, in the other, most obviously by much in the Letters of Paul, and characterized by the terms 'story' and 'doctrine', can only be described as problematic or odd. Not that they have generally seemed so.

What use was to be made of the Gospels? It came to be in order to comment on them, from the time of Origen in the third century. It was not a common pursuit (and still is not, despite the evidence of publishers' catalogues), but it could be embraced by learned and prominent Christians, sometimes with astute and sophisticated results. Nevertheless, though allegorical and symbolic elements might be discerned where appropriate, the dominant perception of the Gospels was as windows giving relatively directly on to Jesus' life and as reservoirs of his divinely authenticated teaching. But the Church's main concern was to preserve and teach the God-given pattern of truth ('doctrine'). The role of the Gospels was to serve that end. Therefore, their dominant use was by way of tags – useful quotations, relevant to current questions or issues. In a modern perspective, much of this simple quoting seems maddeningly frustrating as a way of achieving its aim. Words and sentences are routinely reproduced without any sense that times (and so meanings) had changed since the period when they were written and that they were never designed to address the issues to which they were now being applied. Thus (to take a familiar example), in the fourth century, Arians appealed to John 14.28 ('The Father is greater than I') and the orthodox Nicenes responded with John 10.30 ('The Father and I are one'). To the modern reader, aware of the cultural changes between the world of the Fourth Gospel and that of the fourth-century Church, these appeals were misapplied: the writer of John's Gospel simply did not have his mind on the Arian question and could probably have made little sense of it. But to the Christians of the later period it seemed axiomatic that Jesus, the eternal Word made flesh, was simply speaking directly, in oracular fashion, through the scriptural text. No question of different historical and intellectual contexts arose. The word 'anachronism' was not coined until the mid-seventeenth century!

More specifically from the point of view of this book, quoting was literalist and largely without regard to original contexts, partly because no alternative was intellectually available but decisively because what was involved was 'holy words', given for human instruction in the way of salvation. And in particular, clearly nobody asked: what did Mark (or Matthew, Luke or John) actually think? how did his mind work, and how is it manifested in his book? If they were seen as, in effect, stenographers of Jesus' words (though with the Spirit as delayed intermediary) and, in their own comments, inspired and infallible, then, though there might be ample room for argument about inter-pretation, there was, as a rule, little sense of the Gospel's own original context or that of the evangelist as a man with a mind of his own.

In any case (and this is at first sight surprising), the Gospels have been relatively little quoted, even in Christian writings where one would expect them to figure constantly. For example, in many of the key writings of the patristic age, whose concern is to expound and defend Christian truth ('doctrine'), the texts most often referred to are from the Old Testament, especially the Psalms and the Prophets. Key interests were first to demonstrate that Christianity was not Judaism, or rather was Judaism's fulfilment, and second to show that it was a faith with roots. By contrast with our own time, the ancient world gave little credit to jumped-up novelties. So perhaps it is understandable (though still not wholly so) that the Gospels, in particular Jesus' teaching and deeds, are rarely referred to. If they are, it is often to back a position which, one feels, is held not because of the statement in the Gospels but independently – it stands essentially on its own feet. (This is of course a persisting procedure: 'as Scripture says' frequently backs a view held on other grounds. So we see much more popular reference to vetoes relating to sexual or marital matters than to passages about the abandoning of riches or of family for the sake of the kingdom.) The position seems to be that, while the Gospels were revered in theory, read in liturgy and expounded in sermons, their role in the key matter of stating and defending Christian belief was small. We take examples.

As the heading to this chapter tells us, Justin (mid-second century) says that the Gospels are read in Christian gatherings, but in the work from which the passage comes, his *Apology* or 'defence' of the Christian faith, quotations from the Gospels are virtually limited to Chapters 15 and 16, where he wishes his readers to understand that Jesus 'was no sophist, but his word was the power of God'. There follow samples of Jesus' moral teachings, mostly from Matthew. By contrast, the Old Testament figures constantly throughout the work.

Now it may be thought that the Gospels were regarded as so sacred, so intra-mural to the Christian community, that to parade them prominently in a work designed to commend the faith to outsiders seemed improper. But the use of them in the particular context of an exposition of the moral priorities of Christians belies that. No, it seems that when one was in 'doctrine' mode, the Gospels seemed, to Justin at any rate, not to be serviceable.

He was certainly not alone. In his brief but important work, the *Demonstration of the Apostolic Preaching*, written not for potential converts at all, but to foster the devotion and understanding of the faithful, Irenaeus, bishop of Lyons in the latter part of the second century, makes equally meagre use of the Gospels. In the indices to a standard edition there are four pages of references to Old Testament passages, only one page of Gospel references (over 30 to Matthew, 20 to John, fewer to Luke and a paltry five to Mark).

When we move to the fourth century, we find a considerable development in the intellectual sophistication in which Christian theology was formulated, and it is not surprising that the Gospel of John has moved into greater prominence. As was suggested earlier, this appeal to John was often based upon a reading of its words through more developed (and anyway different) philosophical eyes than those of the evangelist himself; nevertheless, it is easy to see why its idiom and many of its terms were found congenial in doctrinal discussion. Even so, in for instance the major work of Athanasius, *On the Incarnation of the Word*, we find more references to the Old Testament than to the Gospels, and only a handful from the Synoptic Gospels, none of them vital to the argument. Similarly, in the *Address on Religious Instruction* by his younger contemporary Gregory of Nyssa, there are only two or three references to the Synoptic Gospels – or, putting it more bluntly, to the life and teaching of the Jesus who was the mediator and focus of the faith the writer was expounding as pastor. Neither the agenda nor the terms of thought show any concern to focus on the very books that gave most obvious access to what Jesus stood for. In the catechetical *Lectures on the Christian Sacraments* by Cyril of Jerusalem, from the same period, there is, again, scarcely any reference to the Gospels (it is to Matthew alone). Even the narrative of the Last Supper, central to Cyril's subject, is given in the words of Paul in 1 Corinthians 11.23–25 (though the Matthean form of the words over the cup also appears; see Catechesis IV); and the Old Testament continues to predominate, together with the letters of Paul.

The Nestorian controversy of the first half of the fifth century brought uncommon attention to the Gospels, but not, as it were, for their own sake. It was because only they could subserve the interests that divided the Nestorians from their orthodox opponents. The Gospels offered the unique means of distinguishing (or so it appeared) between the activities of the two natures of Christ, the divine and the human, to the establishing of whose distinctness Nestorius was devoted: here, in his weeping at news of Lazarus' death we see the humanity in action; there, in the stilling of the storm, we see the divinity. Improbable as a picture of the workings of any person at all as it may now seem (and as surely it would have seemed to the evangelists), it was a setting in which the Gospels, considered in detail, served a useful purpose – for the sake of the doctrinal enterprise. The theological concepts themselves, unusually, required close attention to the old books about Jesus in the study and the place of teaching as well as in the formality of the liturgy.

It is not long before we find the quoting of gospel texts in a literary or cultural spirit, such as has survived in European culture until only the other day. Here, the texts have turned in effect into proverbs. There is no attention to their original context, much less their intent; only to their rough applicability, by way of happily familiar commonplace, to the situation in hand. For example, in the mid-sixth-century *Rule* of St Benedict, Chapter 60, which concerns the manner of receiving a priest into the monastery, he is to be welcomed with the words of Matthew 26.50, 'Friend, wherefore art thou come?' It is to be hoped that such a priest did not recognize the context of the words (they are those with which Jesus greets Judas at his arrest), or immediate flight might seem the fitting reaction. But there is no sign that this was a deliberate way of discouraging visiting priests, for the passage goes on to recommend the warmest of welcomes. It is rather an early stage in the process that leads us, for example, to dub a worthily busy housewife a proper Martha, or makes us say, sardonically, when the results of a person's activities become plain, 'By their fruits ye shall know them' (Matt. 7.10). In such quoting there is no question of serious exegetical appropriateness; it is simply that the scriptural, indeed dominical words sufficiently fit the circumstances to hit them off a little more memorably than a less gnomic utterance. There was a time when many persons of a certain kind of education peppered their speech with such quotations, with no religious intent.

The *Rule* of St Benedict as a whole, laying out the manner of life to be observed by monks, where it might be thought that the teaching of Jesus would be a primary guide (for Jesus' own manner of life in the company of his disciples is not wholly dissimilar), contains the merest handful of allusions to the Gospels – a great many more to the Psalms. True, the abbot must visit a monk who falls ill because Jesus said, 'I was sick and you visited me' (Matt. 25.36), but it is hard to believe that without the text the sick man would have been left uncared for. In other words, not only is the use of the Gospels beginning to be on the way to culturally proverbial, but also texts are already beginning to be dragged in by the scruff of their necks, serving no very useful purpose, except perhaps to inject a note of piety. In the latter case, they are simply reserves of holy words that may be drawn upon as the spirit moves (itself, of course, a case in point, a degenerate metaphor derived from Gen.1.1). Typically, Benedict gives many more quotations from the Old Testament, where monastic life was never more than remotely in view.

Perhaps the most surprising (if surprise remains) example of all from classical Christian literature concerns Thomas à Kempis' *The Imitation of Christ*, from the early fifteenth-century Netherlands. Again, despite the book's avowed subject, there is much more reference to the Old Testament than to the Gospels; just a few references, few of them vital to the matter in hand, an exception being Book Four, on the Blessed Sacrament. The key lies in the belief that Jesus, God's eternal Word, speaks throughout the Scriptures, as much in the Psalms as in the sayings of the Gospels. The belief even leads to imaginary dialogues with Christ where he speaks to the disciple in terms drawn from all parts of the Bible. In the terms of the time, the doctrine is impeccable, though, for reasons that will be apparent, it is likely to seem to the modern student of the Gospels to be a strange and problematic way of attending to the 'voice' of the Master. At best, we may say that, as commonly, the Gospels are seen in the *Imitation* as collections of material which one might (but not very often) quote as they seem helpful. It is impossible to feel that they were taken seriously as whole books, in their own right. We may even feel that their authors received a raw deal. One would after all think it a prime rule that if you set out to 'follow' a person, you listen to his words as best you can – they are your prime resource, even if they turn out to be more indirect than you wish and than you began by supposing.

If, with these severe limitations, the Gospels were chiefly seen as useful quarries, to be drawn upon if needed (that is, apart from liturgical reading, in the West in a non-vernacular tongue, and preaching), there was a strong inclination to focus heavily (in art, stained glass, music) on certain episodes from Jesus' story, especially the nativity, the passion and the resurrection. Or else to focus meditatively on a single episode and draw from it every atom of nourishment, as, for example, the Martha and Mary story (Luke 10.38–42) in the fourteenth-century *Cloud of Unknowing*. But this moves us into a more popular sphere than the theological or devotional works which have served as our examples.

In Western Christianity, the tendency to use the Gospels in ways that, to say the least, underplay their integrity as works written with a coherent purpose, only to be found by taking them as the deliberate products of the minds of their authors, was accentuated even further in the Middle Ages, and it persisted in certain respects until modern liturgical reforms. Eamon Duffy (1992, pp. 214ff.) describes the use of the Gospels in ways that may strike us as bordering on the magical: the gaining of merit and heavenly protection by hearing the recitation of particular key passages, especially the invoking of the first fourteen verses of the Gospel of John (read until recently in Roman Catholic and many Anglican churches at the end of the mass), together with the kissing of the book and the crossing of oneself. The venerating of the often elaborately decorated Book of the Gospels, used for the reading of the Gospel in the liturgy of the mass, together with the censing of the book before the reading, have, over many centuries, heightened the status of 'the Gospels' as a holy gift of God to his Church, being the story of the Saviour, without their necessarily being heard in an intelligible tongue, studied, or considered, and without a thought of their being other than stores of beneficently sacred words, the greater number of which stayed, for the most part, between the covers. Many passages indeed never found their way into use in the eucharistic liturgy at all.

We have described, even to the point of tedium, the paucity of use made of the Gospels, even in writings which seemed, by their subject-matter, to demand it; and the strange features of their use by later Christian authors, not only in terms of quantity, often by comparison with the Old Testament, but also in character, with passages being quoted out of context or with only doubtful relevance to the matter in hand. The sixteenth-century developments of biblical learning and of lively attention to the text meant changes in this situation. To turn, for example, to

John Calvin's *Institutes* (literally, 'school') *of the Christian Religion* (1536–1559) is to experience a sudden explosion in the extent of reference to the Gospels. It is, however, still a matter of quoting or referring where the subject in hand indicates. Of course the treatment of the subject is affected by the Gospel text; nevertheless it is Calvin's agenda and context that are dominant. In other words, we are firmly in 'doctrine' mode rather than 'story' mode. His purpose is to provide a comprehensive work of instruction in Christian belief, topic by topic, question by question – following, in that way, the mode of the medieval schoolmen, and the style of programme that, as we saw, appeared from the start in the simple credal forms in the New Testament itself. In the English context, at a later stage in the sixteenth century, Richard Hooker's *Laws of Ecclesiastical Polity*, less comprehensive in their theological agenda than Calvin's work, also refer with greater frequency than hitherto to the Gospels, but with similar limitations.

In more recent times, as Christian theology has come to be restated in new contexts of thought, there has been a continuing reluctance to use the Gospels as themselves 'books that emerged from minds'; and still they are quoted as the agenda seems to dictate. A relatively modern and popular example is the widely used *Principles of Christian Theology* of John Macquarrie (1966). As we shall see, such a use (sparing and minimally critical) does little justice to the increasingly independent study of the Gospels over the past two and a half centuries and shows an attachment to the 'doctrine' mode that verges on the axiomatic: this is simply the way to state and discuss the Christian faith. We shall see later that it has limitations and that the 'story' mode, which has always remained in Christian use but often strangely and spasmodically, has possibilities that have lain too long unnoticed. How that awareness came to birth must now be briefly described.

If your concern is to provide a consecutive account of the life of Jesus, then the acceptance of more than one Gospel has always been a problem. Even if only two were in view, their differences made for difficulty: what was to be done about reconciling them? So long as a particular church had only one Gospel, the problem did not arise. But from perhaps as early as the middle of the second century, the four Gospels that have remained 'canonical' were seen, virtually everywhere, as authoritative, and therefore 'true' and accurate tellings of the Lord's story. For that reason, the underlying need for 'Gospel criticism', in one form or another, goes back to that time. What is more, it began to be faced almost immediately, notably in Tatian's attempt (in his *Diatessaron* – 'by means of the four') to produce a single account out of the four. It was the first attempt at making what later came to be known as a 'harmony'. The assumption was that everything in all four was precious and so must somehow be included; and the method chosen was to use the Gospel of John as the framework, into which the episodes in the other three were fitted to make as satisfactory a single account as possible. The primacy of John in this regard is understandable, given the task in hand: with its three passovers, it gave the longest spread of Jesus' ministry, and therefore offered the outline into which everything else should be fitted. Tatian's work survived, but spasmodically, chiefly, though not exclusively, in Syrian and other parts of Eastern Christianity; though the heyday of the publishing of 'Harmonies' was from the fifteenth to seventeenth centuries. Even without the use of formal 'harmonies' of this kind, it was customary in all parts of the Church to treat the Gospels in a harmonizing way: everything had happened and so must be knit together in some way. One must be able to say (is it still not heard?), 'Jesus did x shortly after he did y and z.'

As we shall see, the task of harmony-making and the assumptions behind it came to seem a case of misplaced ingenuity. Though many Christians continue to use the Gospels as if the underlying assumption (i.e. everything in all the Gospels occurred and so fits together somehow) were the plain fact of the matter, since the early nineteenth century the whole subject has come to be viewed in a quite different light. What alternative might be possible?

In such a case, what is involved is nothing less than a profound shift in the picture of the past. The eighteenth-century Enlightenment is most commonly seen as marked by new rigour in the application, to theological as to other questions, of human reason. But the period also saw a new awareness of history and of historical difference. Though there are different opinions on how far back one should trace the growth of this awareness, the period since the eighteenth century is dominant as far as the study of the Bible, including the Gospels, is concerned. It is marked by a discriminating imaginative sympathy in visiting the past.

At the same time, the first phase of modern Gospel study concerned itself with a subject that could be studied in a quasi-scientific literary way: the relationship between the first three ('Synoptic') Gospels. Nevertheless, the historical spirit offered a new freedom to the inquiry. This came more freely into play in the form-critical movement that followed in the early decades of the twentieth century. Here, while attention focused initially on the various types of material found in the Gospels, it moved easily from their literary shapes and structures to their likely place in the life (*Sitz im Leben*) of the early churches in the years before the Gospels were written. The books themselves were seen as collections of stories and groups of sayings of Jesus, used in the various activities of church life, then brought into literary form of a relatively simple kind. Yes, there was of course theological content and motivation – these books were written out of faith rather than a desire to entertain or from a simple biographical interest; but that theological factor was neither elaborate nor dominant in its imprint on the traditional material.

Though it can be traced to the beginning of the twentieth century (in the work on the so-called 'messianic secret' in Mark by William Wrede) and was developed, again with regard to Mark, in the writings of R. H. Lightfoot at Oxford in the 1930s and 1940s, the development of a sense of the evangelists as theological writers of substance has come to prominence only since the 1960s, since when it has grown apace. The transformation in the picture of the Gospels has been startling. First, they appear as works of sophistication rather than simplicity. Second, the writers step forward, no longer as mere dutiful collectors of material about Jesus, but as men of theological substance, each with a distinctive message to convey. Thus, while earlier investigators examined the first three Gospels chiefly from the point of view of their purely literary relationships (however they were seen), now those relationships were, it seemed, a medium for the expression of distinctive theological messages. The successors of Mark (i.e. Matthew and Luke) had written, not simply to include more and different material, and had not altered Mark just for reasons of style or minor correction, but in order to express nothing less than a different message, in each case, about Jesus and the Christian life. These were not books produced lightly (for example, out of a fashion in the writing of Gospels), but out of a distinct and strong theological and religious purpose.

It followed that the Gospels testify to diversity and fecundity in early Christianity of a richness, on a scale, and of a kind, hitherto unrecognized. Now it is true that as early as the late second century, Irenaeus had recognized the distinct 'flavours' of the four Gospels in assigning to each of them one of the symbols of the apocalypse – bull, lion, man and eagle (and Burridge [1994], has, with some strain, used the symbols as a kind of mnemonic in expounding modern perceptions of their distinctive theological 'worlds'). But the recent development has brought before us a new and now inescapable way of viewing the Gospels. In reading them:

- it is a matter of wholes rather than 'bits' or collections of items;
- it is a matter of seeing them as embodying in each case a distinctive and effective 'mind'.

Therefore, we are now faced, by way of the Gospels, with a distinct way of 'seeing' Christian faith: 'story' mode, to go alongside the 'doctrine' mode, that was initiated by Paul and was so long dominant in Christian thinking and prestige. In early Christianity, the two were side by side. It was a movement capable of both modes of expressing its faith. And as far as the Gospels were concerned, while the four shared a mode, each was distinct, and, it seems, at least two of the successors of Mark (i.e. Matthew and Luke) were strongly motivated by their disagreement with him (cf. Luke 1.1–4). So the Gospels can be seen to witness, not just to a mode of the expression of faith, but to a pluralism that had been long muzzled by their being for over eighteen centuries bound together in a unity which the two later writers wrote specifically to counter! Put yourself in the evangelists' shoes and consider your fate: to wait all that time before your voice could be heard. There is of course virtue in ensemble singing as well as solo work; but it is hard to be compelled to the former, as if for ever, when you intended the latter. A strange story indeed. Now we turn to the first soloist.

2

Mark: The Wonderful Outsider

It is the best book for the twenty-first century because it is so utterly subversive ... now at last we see Mark's book again and people have brought it to our attention so that we can read it as it really was.

(Fenton, 2001, p. 57f.)

The most dramatic example of the new perspective which we discussed at the end of the last chapter is the Gospel of Mark. If we could not document the story of this, the first book written about the life of Jesus, we should find it hard to believe. If you have ever tried to be an author, you will know that it is often a depressing business. You may begin with high hopes, with a message or a tale to communicate to the world. You expect to be read and to 'make a difference'. The desire is often vain, in both senses of the word, but most notably because you are likely to be scarcely read at all – even if your book sees the light of day. If you are lucky there may be a review or two, a little money, a few nice comments from friends. All too soon, you hear that your book is remaindered or, perhaps, sold out, never to be reprinted.

It is a dispiriting experience. But if it has been yours, in reality or in imagination, you may be consoled when you contemplate the fate of the author of the Gospel of Mark. He should be the patron saint of ignored or under-appreciated authors. Before we get to the sad tale, we revert to some of the matters discussed in Chapter 1.

Mark's Gospel, first of the four to be written, appeared about AD 70, the identity of the author and the place of writing being uncertain and, for our purpose, not of primary importance. It seems that the book had a relatively wide circulation among the Christian communities, probably at least in Syria and Asia Minor, perhaps further afield. In effect, it was read aloud in church meetings and no doubt had its enthusiasts. It also had its critics. In the 80s, two writers known to us took it as the main basis for similar books of their own: we know them as Matthew and Luke. There is every sign that they grasped Mark's message very well indeed – and decided, each in his own way, to counter it. For reasons that will emerge in Chapters 3 and 4, they disapproved of Mark's teaching. It was not that they failed to understand, nor was it merely that they had more information about Jesus to include. It was a matter of positive disagreement, and they set about attempts to eliminate Mark from use. Of course they failed. For reasons that are largely obscure, but, perhaps because of Mark's supposed affiliation to the apostle Peter (of which 1 Pet. 5.13, perhaps Acts 15.37–39, and the later story of Papias about Mark writing down Peter's reminiscences give hints), Mark's Gospel survived, surely by the skin of its teeth, to find a place in the bound-together collection of four at some date in the middle of the second century (of which the papyrus manuscript 45 is the earliest evidence). From then on it has of course remained secure in the canonical bond, but, as we shall see, it has led an emasculated life. It may not be too much to say, outrageously 'forward' as it seems, that Matthew and Luke were the last people until recent times who grasped Mark's teaching – and so disapproved of it that they were moved to make other provision for the Church, hoping, surely, to remove him from use. If they were thwarted in that purpose, their success, though based on other grounds, was nevertheless considerable. A survey of Mark's fate down the years makes that plain.

In Chapter 1 we examined some of the ways in which the Gospels were used in early Christian writings of a mainly doctrinal kind, and we were struck by the relatively meagre number of their appearances. If now we focus on the references to Mark, the number is reduced almost to zero.

But notice, this neglect of Mark has nothing to do with the disapproval of him that underlies the Gospels of Matthew and Luke. By the later period, there was no question of rejection or disapproval – quite the contrary, Mark was included in the collection of four. Rather, the Gospel of Matthew, now ascribed to the apostle, took precedence. It had clear advantages. It included almost everything to be found in Mark and yet was very much fuller. There was information on subjects like Jesus' antecedents and birth, scarcely touched on by Mark, and above all, with its inclusion of Jesus' teaching on a wide range of subjects, including some relevant to church life, like the disciplining of errant members, it was a great deal more useful. There is no difficulty in seeing why, when the two books are compared in terms of their contents, Mark was sidelined.

To revisit some of the writings referred to in the previous chapter: Justin's *Apology*, from the mid-second century, has a mere couple of rather garbled quotings of Mark; the *Demonstration of the Apostolic Preaching* by Irenaeus has five compared with almost 40 from Matthew. Neither Origen in his *On First Principles* nor Athanasius, in *On the Incarnation*, makes clear reference to Mark (though in a small number of cases it is hard to distinguish him from a parallel passage in Matthew or Luke). The same is true of the latter writer's *Orations against the Arians*, and of the christological writings of Cyril of Alexandria (fifth century and in the same Alexandrian tradition). Of course it is true that Mark has few statements that lend themselves to the theological subject-matter of these writings: one is not surprised to find no references to Wordsworth in a textbook of economics. On the positive side, in the work of Serapion, fourth-century Egyptian bishop, we do find seven references to Marcan passages, as compared with 22 to Matthew. However, the neglect of Mark among Alexandrian writers of the fourth and fifth centuries is the more surprising because Eusebius, in his history of the Church written early in the period, reports that Mark was the first bishop of the church in their city. As a footnote to these statistics, bearing rough testimony to Mark's fate in English culture, *The Oxford Dictionary of Quotations* has five pages of quotes from Matthew, two and a half from Luke, four from John, and a mere half-page from Mark. (The eloquent figure for the Book of Common Prayer is no fewer than 18 pages!)

Later periods do nothing to repair the deficit. *The Imitation of Christ*, for example, quotes Mark only once. (And in the recent *Anglican Catechism* by Edward Norman, which uses the Gospels in a wholly traditional way, Mark figures only twice, with Matthew notching up nine references.) Indeed, the deficit

soon extends to other spheres. So, the first commentary on
Mark does not appear until the early seventh century, the work
of an Irish monk. Even so, it is incomplete, leaving gaps and
often providing the most meagre comment, apparently at will.
It was not published in English translation (from the Latin)
until 1998 (ed. Cahill); but that gives no surprise to readers of
these paragraphs.

Liturgical use of Mark is in line. The gospels for Holy Com-
munion provided in the Church of England Book of Common
Prayer of 1662 and its predecessors were largely taken over from
medieval use. The Passion from Mark is read on two days in Holy
Week, but only two Sunday lections are from Mark (nearly half
are from Matthew, rather fewer from Luke and John). Even on
St Mark's day on 25 April the reading is from the Gospel of John.
A short-hand, motto-like way of referring to Mark's Gospel in
medieval piety was 'recumbentibus' (= 'as they were reclining'),
from Mark 16.14, part of the final passage of the Gospel, 16.9–
20, which was read on Ascension Day and functioned in an almost
charm-like way, standing for Mark as a whole in popular devotion. (Such use of the evangelists has its last fading echo in the
patter-prayer, 'Matthew, Mark, Luke and John, bless the bed
that I lie on', with its various folksy adaptations.) That same
passage was also much valued in the period for its sanctioning of
safe snake-handling and (more practically) exorcism by the
apostles and so by the clergy. As will emerge, it is then ironic that
this favoured passage, used as representative for Mark as a whole,
was no part of the original Gospel and is now widely recognized
as spoiling the message he wished to leave with his readers. It is
a sad tale of indignity upon indignity. The Anglican Alternative
Service Book of 1980 took steps forward; but in the last half-
century, first in the Roman Catholic Church and more recently
in Anglican and, where appropriate, Free Church use, Mark has
at last come into his own, being read, virtually throughout, in
sequence every third year, taking his turn with Matthew and
Luke. It is perhaps the most far-reaching and visible effect of
modern Gospel scholarship in church life. An advocate of Mark
will see it as a belated act of recognition, after 19 centuries of
neglect, putting in the shade the often lamented 50-year eclipse
of the music of J. S. Bach until its revival by Felix Mendelssohn.

As we shall see, this 'total coverage' is marred by the difficulty for all but the most attentive to grasp connections from one week to another and to see themes recurring as the evangelist's mind unfolds.

To Mark belongs the honour of first writing a Gospel, that is, laying out the Christian faith by way of the story of Jesus. Was there a sense in which his act resulted from a failure of nerve, a desire to root faith in a known story of the past, with authoritative statements by Jesus for his followers to appeal to? Or was it inevitable, on ordinary human grounds, that the story be told? It can be argued that, with the letters of Paul and other writings to expound the doctrine, and if present faith in the exalted Christ, seen as soon to return, were truly alive, there was no need to look back to the story. And, as we have seen, to judge from the writings of most of the major theologians from that day to this, many have acted on precisely that premise. When it comes to the statement of faith, the story is, it seems, of negligible use. In simple terms, need Mark have gone to the trouble? As we shall see, it depends partly how one views the book that emerged.

The argument here is that Mark's initiative was more one of mode than of principle. The character of his book is such that it too sets out the faith and preaches the gospel, admittedly in a new medium but one which, in his hands, was far from placing Jesus in a remote past but saw him as still acting and speaking for his own. Not a preserver of the archive, he writes from faith for faith. But it is time to outline, not now the way Mark has been used, but the way he has been studied.

THE STUDY OF MARK

Mark's relative obscurity sprang not only from its brevity and non-apostolic authorship, but from the belief, general from the time of its propagation by Augustine of Hippo, that its obvious similarities to Matthew and Luke were to be explained by its having been written as a kind of epitome or shortened version of the earlier Gospels. It was a not unreasonable theory which at least explained plausibly the synoptic phenomena. Why attend to the summation when the fuller versions were before you?

It was a major development – and decisive for Mark's fortunes – when in 1835 Karl Lachmann turned the traditional theory on its head, proposing that Mark was the first Gospel and was used as their basis and framework by Matthew and Luke. Since then, the theory has, despite rearguard actions, gradually established itself almost universally in scholarly opinion. It has not penetrated deeply into church life, perhaps because it has not seemed important. But 'church life' has thereby deceived itself and, as we shall see, been impoverished. A major development was the freeing of Roman Catholic opinion from a previous official adherence to Matthew's priority, in 1943, in the encyclical *Divino Afflante Spiritu*, an event insufficiently appreciated in wartime Europe, for understandable reasons.

Mark's promotion to the role of originator did not lead to a significant growth in his reputation as a writer or as a 'brain'. The first Gospel was taken as a simple book of no great intellectual profundity, perhaps (as Papias had suggested) representing, virtually in anecdotal form, memories of Jesus' deeds and teaching. Its Greek was not stylish, its social origins clearly unpretentious – as one would expect from a Christian community, whether in Rome (as traditionally believed) or elsewhere, in the latter part of the first century.

The treatment of Mark by the form critics, notably in Bultmann (1921, English translation, 1963), moved matters on. The focus now was on the antecedents of Mark: the brief and surely self-contained episodes of which the book was largely made up. One attended to the shape of the various types of story and envisaged their role in church use in the period of oral transmission that had preceded Mark's decisive act of committing them to written form. On this view, Mark's contribution, though vital, was elementary. It certainly involved no high intellectual achievement. So Bultmann gave only a few pages at the end of his book to Mark's theology. The evangelist was keen to give centrality to Jesus as preacher of 'the kingdom of God', and he used the device known as 'the messianic secret' (to which, as we saw in Chapter 1, Wrede had drawn attention two decades before): that is, you could explain Jesus' puzzling (and surely historically unconvincing) instructions to people not to make him known, by seeing it as a device to account for the failure of Jesus' role as the Messiah of Israel to be known in his lifetime. Wrede's explanation was that the belief only began after the resurrection and was read back by the Church into Jesus' lifetime; so it was clever to show him reticent about it and the disciples as mostly obtuse. On any showing, this was a meagre harvest to put forward as the sum of Marcan theology. Mark remained no intellectual. And as a writer, he was a collector of items, an assembler or editor rather than an author; worthy but not remarkable.

It was therefore a revolution when a picture of Mark came to be put forward which was the very antithesis of this simplicity. Far from being the rather naive anecdotalist of, for example, Alec McCowen's famous (and remarkable) recitations of Mark, which at least had the merit of making his audiences treat the Gospel as a single whole, Mark has come to be seen as a writer of great subtlety and genuine theological power. The substance of such a perception goes back to the work of R. H. Lightfoot (e.g. 1950). It took an extreme form in the almost contemporary work of Farrer (especially 1951), and was continued more soberly in, for example, Marxsen (1961), Hooker (1983), and a great many more studies, which have carried what began as a 'redaction-critical' approach to Mark into an increasingly subtle appreciation of his literary power. For a strong witness to these developments, see Fenton (2001).

We notice an interesting feature of this story of Mark's academic fate in the past century and more. On the one hand, the Synoptic studies, which led to the belief in his priority as an evangelist, gave him instant precedence, and the other evangelists, or Matthew and Luke at least, receded. But, on the other hand, the more recent understanding of him as a writer with a mind of originality and substance puts him into parity with the others (who have of course come to be viewed in the same way). All are people (or books) with a strong and distinctive theologico-religious message to communicate.

Moreover, the method of study affects how one reads the Gospels. On form-critical assumptions the traditional church way of reading them, in brief sections, sandwiched (even if highlighted) between epistle and sermon, makes good sense, for it reproduces the manner of their origins. If Mark was indeed a collection of originally distinct oral items, then to read them so in church was faithful to origins. But if this book (and the other Gospels too) is a work expressive of a single coherent vision, then this is scarcely communicable if it is experienced in short sections at weekly intervals. Moreover, the mind of a mere collector has (as Bultmann illustrated) the limited interest of that evinced in the putting together of the items included in a newspaper: while doubtless having its own place in the inquiries of a student of journalism, it is no place to look for profundity of intellect. But the mind of an evangelist, seen as a man with a vision of his own, is that of an author worth attending to. Alec McCowen's recitation was interesting in communicating, by its single-session character (though with an interval!), the sense of Mark as author, but the message was impeded by an anecdotal mode of speech – almost saying, Oh, I also remember that Jesus…

But how then was Mark intended to be read? Well, probably with solemnity rather than with conversational jauntiness. The oldest manuscripts have the same features as those found in the Jewish Scriptures, notably the signalling of 'holy names' (Jesus, God, Lord, Son, etc.) so that they may be read or chanted with special reverence. Those used to welcoming more 'realistic' and hearer-friendly readings of the Scriptures in church may ponder the thought that Mark (and his companions) may well have been chanted, perhaps from the start, in ways of which the departed practice of the Western high mass is a closer descendant than their own preferred practice. Moreover, the greater the internal interconnectedness (e.g. of theme or word-usage), the greater the likelihood that it was meant to be read and heard at a sitting (or perhaps, more usually, a standing). The modern recitations, commonly held in the comfort of a theatre, demonstrate that it is in our day by no means out of the question; though such a thought can bring no comfort to the designer of liturgy.

It has long been assumed (and we saw that form-critical ideas chimed in with ease) that Mark was from the start meant for quasi-liturgical use of some kind. But truly, we have no solid evidence how these matters were handled in his circle about

AD 70. Justin, in the mid-second century, tells us that at the eucharistic assembly, the apostles' memoirs (= the Gospels) were read as long as was convenient. We do not know how long that might be: it would depend, presumably, what else people had to do. It is evident that the content of the liturgy itself was at least as full as it is now; but perhaps there was less need to 'rush off' – but would that be so, for many, in a context where Sunday was a working day? Perhaps in practice, Mark (where lucky enough still to be used) was already, by Justin's day, reduced to 'snippets' – whatever Mark's original intentions and hopes had been. We shall see later that perhaps other evangelists had taken more realistic account of these matters.

There is an objection to the current sense of Mark as a person of substantial intellectual subtlety. It concerns his Greek – which is simple to the point of crudity. But in the Mediterranean world of his day, Greek was a lingua franca with some of the properties of English in the modern world: a language spoken in a wide variety of ways by a wide variety of people, differing in native culture, intelligence and education. Not all the bright people who today speak English use the standard idioms of high-grade English education. In Mark's world, even more, intelligence was not always matched by education or training in the art of writing. In fact, as was suggested in the last chapter, Mark shows signs of a certain level of formal attainment in the crucial subject of rhetoric: hence his repetitions of words and themes, often in patterns that make for easy memorability. His talents were not those easily recognized by the modern silent reader, nor can the modern hearer appreciate them for want of being attuned to them; but that need not make us discount their existence, and we can learn to recognize them.

A measure of ability to write convincing Greek (at least as far as his own audience was concerned) was not this writer's only gift. He had also achieved some confidence in the use of the old Jewish Scriptures. He can quote them, though he does not do it often, and he can allude to key episodes and images; and he could expect his hearers to chime in with them. That implies that the Scriptures (or parts of them) were current in the Christian circles to which he belonged; and it confirms the impression that while there was substantial gentile membership of the Church by AD 70, the Jewish contribution retained presence or at any rate influence even when only few were of Jewish race and background. Recognition of a repertory of scriptural stories could be counted on, even if referred to by only a single word. Thus, Mark's insertion of the word 'beloved' into the quotation of Psalm 2.7 in the baptism story at 1.11 may well recall the Septuagint (Greek) version of the story of Isaac's near-sacrifice in Genesis 22: the word is there reiterated to bring out the special status of Abraham's precious son and heir, on whom the promised future wholly depended. Paul (Rom. 8.32) had already called upon that story to illuminate the role of Jesus, who was not 'spared' and who too was the single thread on whom salvation hung. Whether Mark himself was of Jewish or gentile origin is not clear, but a degree of scriptural formation is beyond question; and the ranks of the 'God-fearers' are bound to spring to mind, that is, gentiles who had associated themselves with the synagogue, impressed by its piety, venerability of tradition, and respect for learning and the study of its texts. It is virtually certain that such persons were prominent among the converts of, in particular, the Pauline mission (and see the numerous references in Acts, easily missed, to people who 'feared' or 'worshipped' God, e.g. 10.2; 16.14; not to mention the 'half-breed' Timothy, 16.1).

Moreover, it has often been noticed that Mark shows a number of signs of being marked by Pauline Christianity. In addition to the example given above, we can point to their shared use (virtually unique among the New Testament writers) of the word 'gospel' to signify the Christian message (e.g. Mark 1.1; 8.35; 14.9); the use of the symbols of baptism and cup for Jesus' passion in 10.38, recalling Paul's understanding of baptism and eucharist in terms of union with Jesus' death (Rom. 6.3–11; 1 Cor. 10.16; 11.26). And, as we shall see, Mark's sense of the universal need for salvation by an act of sheer grace is nothing less than a presentation of Paul's doctrine in vivid narrative form.

THE BOOK

There is no need to provide an outline of the contents of Mark's Gospel. It is brief, easily read and, as it seems, accessible. But it is necessary to decide its limits, in particular where it comes to an end. It is now virtually universally believed that verse 8 of chapter 16 is where Mark meant to stop, unsatisfactory as it is likely to seem to the reader. Dramatic thoughts of the writer being seized from his sacred task by violent soldiery as he penned the words 'for they were afraid', and being unable to go further, have vanished into the abyss. What is clear is that the modern sense of the unfinishedness of the work at that point was already felt within a few decades, and more satisfactory endings were composed, giving a decent (though in other ways unattractive) sense of closure. Hence 16.9–20, which established itself within the canonical text (and so to this day retains a stubborn presence in many editions). Hence also alternative endings with the same purpose; and indeed the endings soon supplied by Matthew and Luke as they worked with Mark as their basis, and recoiled, surely with mystification and dismay, when they reached 16.8 and felt that something must be done. Let us then decide: like it or not (and perhaps we can learn to like it), that is the extent of the book.

The decision leads us to an intensified perception of the Gospel as dominated by the passion; for the resurrection barely appears, except in promise, and we are thus prevented from escaping the death of Jesus into Easter joy. Jesus reaches Jerusalem, and the process that leads to that death begins in 11.1. But it has already long been on the agenda. Obviously in 3.6, and then in Jesus' own prophecies, repeated with rhetorical emphasis, at 8.31, 9.31 and 10.32–34. Less plainly, unless you have the right kind of ear, in 1.11 (see above); and in the temptation in 1.13–14, which presages Gethsemane. The long narration of the passion and death of John the Baptist, herald and baptizer of Jesus, in 6.14–29 gives a clearer sign of what is to come. And Peter's bungling 'faith' in 8.29, which leads with startling speed to his identification with Satan (v. 33), is a sign of the abandonment of Jesus by his followers that is soon to come.

This focusing on Jesus' death is yet another sign of Pauline doctrine. For him too it was the crucial episode of Jesus' career, and by no means something to be put behind now that his exaltation had come. The death was the means to sin's end and the sign of love (cf. Mark 10.45; Gal. 2.20).

There being then no division into chapters and verses, we cannot tell how Mark saw a plan in the work. Farrer (1951) thought his arrangement of episodes was esoteric in the extreme. If he was wrong in his particular suggestion, he is less likely to be wrong in principle: Mark may have had some kind of mnemonic to work by. Alternatively, he may, as earlier critics felt, have just done his best to set down in a reasonable order the stories that had come his way. But it would be simplistic to discard all sense of plan. It is surely undeniable that his picture is dominated by the idea of purposive journey; in essence from Galilee, where all good is done, to Jerusalem, where death is imposed, but with the promise, left in the air, of Galilee still to come (14.28; 16.7).

The image of a journey is among the most hackneyed in the armoury of preachers and of many others hoping to edify their neighbours. Mark himself was drawing on a symbol that lay deep in Jewish consciousness: the Exodus from Egypt was the people's foundation story, itself foreshadowed by Abraham's journey from Haran to the land of promise; and the experience was painfully renewed by the Babylonian captivity and the return – and by hopes of a future greater return of an increasingly dispersed race. It was also a myth familiar to instructed pagan consciousness, in the story of Odysseus (for its possible influence, see MacDonald, 2000).

In Mark, its importance is to be seen in the repeated use of the word 'way' (*hodos*). It is the key to the selection of the two opening texts from Isaiah and Malachi (1.2–3), linked together by their common use of that word, which therefore characterizes the work of Jesus from the start. (So it indeed appears that Mark wanted to give us more than a random collection of inherited anecdotes.) It appears again in 4.4, 15 (RSV has 'path' – diverting us from Mark's device). And 10.46 uses the very same phrase, balancing it in v. 52. To be 'off the way' is useless; to 'follow in the way' is salvation indeed. Or, at any rate, it is, as we say, to be on the right track. We may note that in Isaiah 35.5, the healing of the blind is, as elsewhere, a prime metaphor for salvation, and in v. 8 we find: 'And a highway shall be there, and it shall be called the holy way' (*hodos* in the Septuagint both times). Jesus himself, naturally, is 'in the way' (10.32) – towards

Jerusalem, where his destined work lies. It is no wonder that Mark sees Jesus as in a hurry: 'immediately' (*euthus*) occurring 43 times. That haste accords with the necessity of Jesus' work: 'the Son of man must suffer' (8.31). We should note that this is therefore very far from hackneyed use of the image: 'life's journey, with its ups and downs'; or the more purposeful picture of life as ever upward and onward, with growth and achievement coming with experience, leading to greater scope, usefulness and wealth. (At the establishing of the Anglican diocese of Calcutta in 1813, with responsibility for all India, a clergyman offered his services, so that he might extend his 'very extensive field for usefulness'. It was not quite Mark's sense of the calling of Jesus.)

All the same, though the purpose was to endure a saving death, which would be 'a ransom for many' (10.45), and Mark does all he can to head off inclinations to divert attention from it, the promise of 'Galilee' (16.7) gives a hint of more and better to come (though it must not endanger the priority, for now, of what precedes). At the same time, both through suffering and then on to Galilee, the role of others is to 'follow'. In particular stories, the word belongs, as it seems, within the terms of that episode, e.g. 2.14; 10.52. But it is also paradigmatic, even if, as in the case of Levi, 2.13–14, the one who follows never appears again. In the case of Bartimaeus, 10.52, even though he does not recur, his new seeing and his following lead immediately to Jerusalem and the passion. In the word's first and perhaps normative use, in the call of the first four disciples (1.16–20), there is the complication that, follow as they do, ambiguity appears and intensifies, until they cease to follow, in the abandonment of 14.50. There is fear in following, in 10.32, and Peter's 'following' after the arrest is at a safe distance – 'from afar' (14.54). Yet there is the hint of light, as restoration is promised in 16.7.

That following is to be marked by suffering (which is the vocation of Jesus) and by loss comes before us in terms of the taking up of the cross (8.34, implicitly declined by Peter already two verses before, and explicitly in the denial and abandonment in the passion itself, where Simon of Cyrene replaces him in that very role, 15.21). That it is to be marked by loss (of family and possessions) is explicit in 10.28–31 (as in the exemplary passages, 1.16–20 and perhaps 2.13–14), and even the reward of membership of the new community of the Church will come 'with persecutions'.

Mark's term for those 'followers' who recur in the narrative is 'disciples', i.e. pupils. That is, Jesus teaches them. (Despite the fact that, having Matthew and Luke also before us, we tend to see Mark as short on teaching material, in one form or another almost a third of Mark's space is devoted to it, and he uses the verb 'teach' (*didasko*) more often than Matthew and as often as Luke, and the noun 'teaching' more often than either.) Yet the use of this language is strange. Though other individuals might draw pupils to themselves (e.g. John the Baptist and perhaps leading Essenes), the rabbinic pattern was for a pupil to attend a teacher-rabbi as long as seemed fruitful: the pupil's loyalty was not to the man but to the Law, the Torah, the object of study. One learnt and moved on. In the case of Jesus, according to Mark, on the contrary, the follower was meant to stay (it is implicit in 1.16–20 and in the commissioning of the Twelve at 3.13–19); and yet they abandon him (14.50). Their role, as disciples, is to learn (implicit in the phrase 'to be with him', as at least part of its sense, 3.14): and yet they fail to do so (6.52; 8.17; 10.35–45). They neither 'see' nor 'hear', despite their having been 'given the secret of the kingdom of God' (4.10). In this way, Mark is disturbing to those who read or hear him. Is this where following Jesus gets you – to ignorance and failure, and, even if you were to 'do it right', to death? And was this then one of the reasons why this Gospel was felt to need to be improved upon? For surely there might be such a thing as successful discipleship, the earning of one's reward. As we shall see, the writer of the Gospel of Matthew certainly thought so. There is another refinement. We can say that the task of 'learning' from Jesus was implicit in what Mark says about the disciples' failure to understand; but he never uses the verb 'learn' (except once, irrelevantly for this purpose, at 13.28). Rather, as we have seen, in the 'school' of Jesus (if we can call it that at all), the pupils' task is less to learn than to follow or to 'come after' Jesus (8.34): that is, the metaphor of the journey is paramount.

What has been said so far in this section surely justifies the description of a Gospel (or this one at least) as the statement of Christian faith by way of the story of Jesus (as distinct from concepts or patterns of abstract ideas). Mark's book is far from being merely a literary exercise. It is a theologico-religious statement. Of course it has identifiable literary features, and in what follows we shall draw on strands in the study of Mark which emphasize them. Since the boom in Marcan studies of a theological kind got under way during the past forty years, there have in fact been two distinguishable tendencies at work. Both agree that the book is the work of an author rather than a mere collector of items; both agree that he has a doctrinal message to communicate, a perception of Jesus as the decisive agent of God which is both subtle and powerful. However, many critics never lose sight of the historical context, both in the realities of first-century life and within the circumstances of the Christian community, so far as it is visible through its various literary remains (Beavis, 1989, falls into this category, for example); while others, with a 'pure' literary approach in mind, give an account of the text that is much more 'timeless' in its analysis (see for instance Rhoads, Dewey and Michie, 1999). In some of what follows, we shall endeavour to profit from the second without losing sight of the constant presence of the first: for in this book, the wider picture of early Christianity is implicit throughout, however obscure it often is. It is a matter of thoughts that began in human heads in human bodies in human societies.

The people in the Gospel

We turn now to other features of the Gospel of Mark. Many of them have in recent years come to be widely recognized, though there can be disagreement about particular instances. The first was well documented by Rhoads and Michie (1984), and it makes an intriguing refutation of those impressed by the supposed breathless ('immediately') simplicity of Mark.

We have already drawn attention to the failure and inadequacy of the disciples which has often seemed such a surprising and even embarrassing aspect of the Gospel. As we shall see, Matthew and Luke both felt it to be so and were at pains to improve their image at almost every opportunity. However, it is necessary to put this depiction in a wider context. For the truth is that the disciples do not stand alone in being painted negatively. The same applies, less surprisingly, to the scribes and Pharisees (indeed to the Jewish leaders in general) and (more doubtfully) to Jesus' family. What these groups have in common, as far as the Gospel is concerned, is that they recur, with varying frequency, throughout the work. It is less clearly true of the family, but it is sufficiently true to conform to the 'rule' which appears to emerge.

By contrast, the characters who appear only once in the narrative, for example a blind man who is healed or a child whose life is restored, are uniformly (though with one apparent exception) figures who are pictures of faith or else of the reception of God's saving gift. While the first group are, as it were, cautionary examples to the reader, the second are models with whom to identify. In life, we live among circles that differ in nearness to us – e.g. family and friends, then work associates, then casual acquaintances. In a play like Shakespeare's *Twelfth Night*, there are people from the higher and then from the lower levels of the society in question, and the same is true of *A Midsummer Night's Dream* and the Falstaff plays. In Mark, there is a comparable division, but it is made not on grounds of social position but of the nature of the response given to Jesus; yet it is similar to Shakespeare in that each is a foil to the other.

We examine Mark's two groups in turn, and first those who are, in varying degrees, failures in relation to Jesus and his cause (i.e. the promotion of the kingdom of God); those to whom the reader is surely supposed to say, 'No, I do not wish to be of their company.'

Scribes and Pharisees

We now recognize that, in the light of history, the depiction of the scribes and Pharisees is unjust: its negativity is, in its unremitting quality, artificial. Bluntly, they were not, as whole classes, reprehensible persons by any reasonable standards. Doubtless, Jesus had controversies with these (and other Jewish) groups, but it would be surprising if it were as constant and as 'black-and-white' as the Gospel implies. Only in 12.28–34 does a scribe show, as we might put it, any sign of grace, and we now realize that, as Mark tells it, it is not so much a case of his being affected by Jesus and moving beyond scribal teaching as of Jesus seeking to make him face its true implications. It is therefore less an exception to the rule than it appears at first sight. In the case of scribes, the hostility carries straight through to the passion, where they play a leading part. So these groups represent, in Mark's narrative, negativity towards Jesus at its strongest. We shall see that the other evangelists had no difficulty in accepting and amplifying this doctrine.

The disciples

As we have seen, this is a more ambiguous group – as we should expect. With the parable of the sower (4.1–20) providing a kind of guide to the matter (and indeed more widely), we see these people, who are called and who follow, failing repeatedly, first in their grasp of Jesus' role and purpose, and then in plain loyalty or faith. And in the naked ambition of 10.35–45, we go beyond the failures of cowardice or obtuseness to moral crudity. Despite their reception of Jesus' call and of the gift of the 'secret' (4.10), they are lost in fog and failure. For the hearer or reader, compared with the scribes, the disciples are closer to home. Equally, however, they serve as warning. They certainly do not edify or encourage.

The family of Jesus

The family of Jesus too give no impetus for imitation. At 3.21f. they judge Jesus to be mad, so far are they from grasping his mission, and at 3.31–35 their peremptory demand to see him is refused, for they are not of his circle. As in 10.28–31 (a passage where the painful ambiguity of being a 'follower' is clear), the true family of Jesus and indeed of those who turn to him consists of the community around him. At 6.1–6, Jesus is rejected by his home village, including, it seems, his family who are part of it and belong there; or, at least, there is not a hint of their being an exception to the villagers' rejection. At the very least, it would be hard to set in hand the cult of Mary on the basis of the Gospel of Mark (other evangelists were, as we shall see, more co-operative).

The final possible reference is more controversial, and on it depends a claim that, as with the other groups, Jesus' family are depicted throughout the Gospel in a negative way. In the final passages of the work, we encounter the women (three in number) who witness Jesus' death (but, like Peter before the trial, 'from afar', 14.54, with identical words in Greek and indicating detachment from what they see); then two see the place of burial; and finally three go to the tomb 'when the sabbath was past', and receive the young man's news and instructions – which they proceed to disobey (15.40—16.8). The names of the women are, puzzlingly, not the same in the three cases. In particular, in the first we have 'Mary, the mother of James the younger and of Joses'; in the second, 'Mary, the mother of Joses'; and in the third, 'Mary, the mother of James'. It seems over-cautious, however, to deny that the three are meant to be one and the same. The greater difficulty comes when these references are put alongside the description of Jesus in 6.3 as 'the son of Mary and brother of James and Joses and Judas and Simon'.

The question arises whether this does not point to the later Mary being the same as the Mary of the earlier passage; and if that were so, why Mark has expressed himself so cryptically, or at least so inexplicitly. We can suppose (but it is more a hunch than an argument) that Mark's original hearers had information not known to us. And, not surprisingly, critics have tended to find it incredible that Mark would refer to the mother of Jesus in this dark and even offhand way – though that is, of course, to judge Mark in the light of later Christian doctrine and devotion, and as we have seen in the case of the disciples, such an assumption cannot be made. But, if we are on the right lines in seeing the family of Jesus as (for whatever reason) one of the groups presented throughout the Gospel in at least an ambiguous light, then what is being suggested for the identifying of Mary of the final passages as Jesus' mother is what we should expect. And to judge from the not dissimilar case of the disciples, we should perhaps seek a quasi-theological and literary rather than a historical explanation. That is, Mark had no special information to lead him to this picture of either group (except perhaps the tradition of the disciples' flight in the final crisis and the family's non-involvement in Jesus' work and mission), but uses both as parts of his design: they are warnings to us his Christian hearers, the disciples for failure to comprehend and to stick, the family for failure to see what stares them in the face and, at the resurrection, to receive the most clear and hopeful of instructions. (At the same time, the case of the women is, perhaps abruptly, mitigated: they had both 'followed' and 'served' (cf. 1.31) Jesus in Galilee, 15.41.)

These are dire warnings indeed. (For arguments against this identification of the Mary of the final chapters with Jesus' mother, see Catchpole [2000], Chapter 1.) Finally, if we think in terms of 'traditions', we recall that the more independent Gospel of John at least placed the mother of Jesus by the cross (19.25–27); so was it a tradition that Mark was seen to have first recorded?

The 'little people'

The 'little people' of Mark's Gospel, that is those who make only a single appearance, stepping on and off the stage yet contributing to a total picture, can be more quickly described. They range from people healed, for example the blind men who bracket Jesus' journey to Jerusalem (8.22–26 and 10.46–52) – so making a point about the 'sight-bringing' purpose of that journey; to those who appear in the passion: the widow whose selfless generosity leads her to give her all (like Jesus, and like – it is hoped – those who follow him) (12.41–44); and then, within the closer narrative of Jesus' suffering, pre-eminently the woman whose similar generosity is directed so lavishly to Jesus and who receives unique commendation (14.1–9); and Simon of Cyrene, who does in reality what Peter (and the other disciples) was enjoined to do in metaphor (8.34) yet failed to do (15.21); and the centurion-executioner who was moved to confess faith by the spectacle of Jesus' death (15.39). Such people are examples for believers who hear or read this book. More obscure is the significance of the 'young man' who appears at Jesus' arrest (14.51–52) and at his tomb (16.7) (supposing, that is, that Mark means them to be one and the same). Does Mark mean us to see in him the Christian neophyte who shares in the 'stripping' of his death and the knowing of his resurrection (as, in a different, proleptic way, does Jairus' daughter, raised from the dead, 5.21–43)? If so, it seems to have been so much a local Marcan secret that the other evangelists cut out the 'young man's' first, more puzzling appearance, and, in the case of the second, promoted him to angelic status.

There is an apparent exception to what otherwise seems to be a Marcan principle, that the 'single-appearance characters' are for our edification: the rich man who fails at the test that Jesus puts before him, the renunciation of his wealth (10.17–22). John Fenton, in the passage quoted at the head of this chapter, thinks otherwise. He notes that here alone in Mark we read of Jesus loving somebody (v. 21). Jesus 'loves the person who can't do it... We see the impossibility of the demand, "Destroy your life! That's the only way to preserve it." And we know we can't do it, but the man who couldn't do it was the one that Jesus loved' (Fenton, 2001, p. 57–8). It may then be that we have here one of Mark's deepest signs of his Pauline formation: the love of God is bestowed freely and not on the basis of our deserts or performance. The story could be a vivid comment on Romans 5.8: 'God shows his love for us in that while we were yet sinners Christ died for us.'

'Grain-cum-bread': a recurring symbol

We turn to another example of a pervasive feature of Mark, whose significance is cumulative. It is the matter of grain-cum-bread (less easily identified in an urban culture). Here is an excellent example of Mark's rhetorical quality: a recurring theme or symbol for hearers to register and allow to build up in thought and imagination. As with the characters in Mark's drama, some references have a positive, others a negative 'feel'. In the former category, we have the marginalizing of sabbath duty by Jesus' fiat in 2.23–28. (Note: our concern is not with the historical probabilities surrounding such an episode, for instance, whether Jesus' judgement was as out of line as Mark suggests, but only with what Mark wishes us to hear.) Also, the crumbs from the table that betoken the gentile woman's successful claim to be 'fed' in 7.24–29; and the two feedings of crowds (6.30–44; 8.1–13). There are also the sowings that vary in their success in the parable of 4.1–20, together with the amazing fecundity in the subsequent parable of the seed that grows secretly (4.26–29). In all these instances, there is a measure of mystery: we simply cannot see what is finally the meaning. What is at stake? Why are people to be fed by Jesus? And what is the nature of the fruitfulness that is to be expected? In so far as there is explanation, it comes in the Last Supper, where there is, however, still ambiguity. That relates to the two-sidedness of the disciples who share the meal. Still, there is a positive side: Jesus eats with his disciples and they share his bread, whose meaning turns out to be involvement in his death which is his purpose and the 'point' of the kingdom for which he stands. This eating marks the disciples' incorporation into this meaning, despite all that follows in the near future (though, for us readers, there remains the promise in 14.28 and 16.7).

A negative side is also visible, for example in the sower's failures, which are then illustrated in human examples: Peter ('the rock') exhibits the characteristics described in 4.17; and the rich man those of 4.18–19 (cf. 10.17–21); while on the other hand, the minor characters discussed above illustrate the ample fruit of the seed that fell on good soil which in Mark (but not Matthew who draws the Church's bounds more tightly, cf. 12.30 versus Mark 9.40) is ever more abundant (4.8, 20; contrast Matt. 13.8, 23). There are also the disciples' repeated failures to understand the meaning of Jesus' indiscriminate feedings, where bread is a free gift (6.52; 8.14–17). And the Last Supper is followed by the flight from the scene of the arrest (14.50), together with Judas' act of handing over and Peter's act of denial. Again, there are here echoes of Pauline doctrine concerning the bread of the eucharist. It is a free gift, a means of grace. It is a means of association with Christ's death. It carries an obligation of fidelity and corresponding perils where fidelity fails (1 Cor. 10.16–17; 11.23–29).

We may note, in connection with this tendency in Mark to 'theologize' matters that may be treated in other ways, that he is also inclined to view what others see as ethical issues in terms of central theological convictions. Thus, the transcending of sabbath in 2.23—3.6 is not a matter of mere ritual observance or legal obligation, but rather a fruit of Jesus' mission to proclaim the kingdom of God. As in the work of Paul, it is the coming of a whole new dispensation, centred on Christ, that relativizes the Law and then makes its observance by Christians not only unnecessary but so misleading as to lead to apostasy (cf. Gal. 4.8–11). Similarly in relation to divorce, Mark tells of Jesus' veto; but the ground is not legal or narrowly ethical, but doctrinal. The coming of Jesus and entry into the kingdom mean a movement behind the Mosaic dispensation and a restoration of Eden. To hold to the former is a symptom of 'hardness of heart', for Mark a major sin – which the disciples also exhibit, 8.17. To recognize the latter is to enter a new world (or a restoration of God's original creative purpose: compare the paradisal imagery in Revelation 21—22). Though Paul does not bring such a vision into play when discussing divorce, it is certainly part of his doctrine and central to his vision (2 Cor. 5.17; Gal. 6.15).

Finally, though the passion story has figured a number of times in the various topics we have discussed, it should be looked at in its own right and in context. We have seen how central to Mark's picture is the death of Jesus. It is the goal of his 'way' and the necessity which lies upon him (8.31). Of course there is a 'beyond': the Galilee of 16.7, whose precise sense (geographical or symbolic for the Christian movement and its future?) is obscure, and then an assured return of Jesus in triumph. We note that, though judgement figures in Mark, it is in relation to people's response to Jesus (e.g. 12.1–12), and in that way related to Christology. It does not figure explicitly in the picture of the End in chapter 13. There are certainly terrifying aspects of Christ's return, but they are not formally linked to any kind of assize (as so prominently in Matthew). Rather, they serve to impress us with the awesomeness of the destiny which centres on Jesus. But even here, the passion figures prominently – by allusion. It has long been recognized how many features of Mark 13 point ahead to chapters 14—15: e.g. perhaps the boy at the arrest in v. 16; the trial of Jesus as prefiguring those of his followers later in vv. 9–12; the notes of time in v. 35, corresponding to those in the passion story; and the injunction to 'watch' in vv. 32–37, foreshadowing

Gethsemane in 14.32–42. These features help us to see Mark's possible reasons for placing his picture of the larger future here, before the passion, rather than at the end of his book, as its climax. God's purposes for the world will indeed be fulfilled, but the central episode is the death of Jesus, and everything has to be subordinated to that. We note that there are distinct signs of at least a measure of closure in 15.38–39, as words from the Gospel's opening are repeated: the 'splitting' of the heavens at 1.10 is recollected in the splitting of the temple's curtain (a repetition ignored by Matthew and by many translators who prefer the less violent 'open') and 'son of God', not common in Mark, is at 1.11 and then on the centurion's lips. Yet the closure, Mark recognizes, is, though crucial, not complete; so there is more, but again we must not be deflected by it from the centrality of the passion.

Whatever Mark has done to make meaningful history (in that sense, a Christian myth) out of the 'plain' story of Jesus (whatever such a thing could possibly have been like!), he has held to the bedrock fact of Jesus' death as the centre and climax of his story. In that, history and theology coincide. It provides the context in which to see the End, rather than a description of the End, or indeed of the resurrection, being the climax in relation to which Jesus' death might be seen as no more than a vital step. Hence, Mark makes Jesus' death his climax, the end of his 'way', in more senses than one.

Once more, we discern here the perspective of Paul, for whom too the End is 'real', but Jesus' mission is decisive in shifting balances and changing the direction of history, and his death is the heart of what one 'joins' in baptism and relates to in the eucharist (Rom. 6.1–11; 1 Cor. 10.16–17). In this perspective, one's own death (though creating problems of understanding, as Paul found, 1 Thess. 4; 1 Cor. 15) is but an incident in a process whose decisive turning point (death and resurrection) came in baptism. In this sense, the later preoccupation of the Church with death, its preparation and its pomps, was an extraordinary shift of perspective. The corollary of Paul's (and Mark's) view may be that interest in what happens 'after death' is not only fruitless but wrong: in the passion of Jesus is our 'end', and the rest is unknowable and a matter of sheer gift. In that way, it is like

'Galilee' in Mark 16.7: undefined and unidentified, but to be trusted wholly.

In the passion story, as has frequently been noticed (see Vanstone, 1982), Jesus' progress is depicted as increasingly negative; he becomes more and more the passive victim. This shows itself in the frequent use of the verb 'to hand over' (*paradidonai*), coming ten times in the passion story as Jesus is transferred from one group to another (as well as earlier of John the Baptist, the forerunner, and disciples, the successors (1.14; 13.9)). Both Vanstone and, more recently and decisively, Klassen (1996) have taught that it is erroneous to translate the verb by 'betray': its sense is more neutral and its purpose is to impress us with Jesus' passivity. Similarly, he is more and more alone: first, within the Gethsemane episode, going ahead from the twelve with the three and then beyond the three; and then his isolation is emphasized further by the abandonment at the point of the arrest, by Peter and later the women observing from a distance, and by the absence of all support in a setting of increasingly crude hostility; and it is brought out further by his deepening silence, broken finally by his dying cry. Isaiah 53.7 is not quoted (only Acts 8.32 does that in so many words), but it is hard not to believe that it is in mind. Jesus takes the role of sacrificial victim, cf. 10.45. Both the disciples in 14.12, who virtually drag speech out of Jesus, and, more obviously, the centurion, who receives the gift of discernment, are brought towards the execution of God's purpose for them in the midst of Jesus' silence. Similarly, it is out of the women's silence that the disciples will 'see' Jesus in Galilee.

It is worth asking where Mark placed the boundaries of that group. In particular, did it include or exclude Judas, 'the hander-over'? Both Matthew and Luke describe his death, albeit in different ways. Mark says nothing on the subject, beyond the 'woe' of 14.21. Klassen tells us that this ominous word is less disastrous than we may suppose. It is in any case less drastic than Peter's designation as Satan at 8.33, and nevertheless he is singled out for seeing Jesus again in Galilee. Will Judas then, in Mark's picture of the good news, be included? As far as his narrative goes, there is no reason to exclude him. We should recall Paul's doctrine: 'all have sinned and lost the glory of God'

(Rom. 3.23), and remember the inclusiveness of 1 Corinthians 15.22: 'as in Adam all die, so in Christ shall all be made alive'. Could a Pauline Christian exclude Judas? And if he did exclude Judas, why not Peter – and almost everyone, on one ground or another? (In past times, such a view of Judas has been taken not infrequently from a theological point of view. But see Edwin Muir's poem, 'The Transfiguration' [Muir, 1960, p. 198], which takes up the point, with great power).

Learning from Mark

We have been entering into some of the workings of Mark's decision to write out his faith in terms of the story of Jesus. In the circumstances of his writing, we could ask: what did people learn as a result of repeatedly hearing Mark's book? Or, if that is too cerebral a way of putting it, what was the likely effect of this communication in 'story' mode? But we can only judge from our own time; and our tendency is to restate the effect in 'doctrine' mode; e.g. Mark teaches us that Jesus is Messiah, Son of God, Son of Man – as indeed he very clearly does (1.1, 11; 8.31; 10.45; 14.62; etc.). And much can be written on what he is likely to have meant by those terms, leading to an understanding of what we define as 'Mark's Christology'. But the question then is whether that is not to misunderstand his achievement, by converting it into something approaching 'doctrine' mode (though historically sensitive, no doubt). It is a reflex, conditioned by centuries of according privilege to that mode (as Mark's reputation itself helps to testify). He does indeed 'teach' these things, but he does it in the context of the story and gives no sign of thinking we would do well to pluck them out for examination in order to understand them better.

The meditative tradition in Christianity has of course been used to reflecting, with a view to prayer, upon the Gospel stories (though not usually upon Mark); but that tradition has not been used to entering into the structure and flow of a whole narrative, in order to grasp its communication and reflect upon it. It has preferred to imagine with historical realism – in a way that bypasses much that now presses upon our consciousness (those times were not like our times). Yet such an 'entering' is implicit in Mark's achievement and is at its heart. That it is also, in certain ways, 'subversive' (to use John Fenton's word) is an added bonus, given our tendency to lapse into complacency.

3

Matthew: The Bringer of Order

> Matthew writes with broad catechetical and pastoral concerns: he sets out the story and significance of Jesus in order to assist Christians to come to terms with their identity.
>
> (Stanton, 1992, p. 3)

For all his devotion to order, clarity and definiteness, the author of the Gospel of Matthew was, like Mark his half-loved mentor, dedicated to the mode of 'story' for writing out his faith concerning Jesus. His Jewish culture was after all used to expressing itself in narrative: its Scriptures were full of it and its non-scriptural writings continued the tradition; and Matthew's combination of law-like teaching and narrative in a single work follows the example of the Pentateuch and perhaps Deuteronomy in particular. His method – of writing from the starting point of an existing book, and rewriting and amplifying it in order to give a new message – was of course wholly traditional. Scripture consisted mostly of works produced in such a way, combining respect for the inheritance with determination not to rest with it. We think of the layers of the Pentateuch or of Isaiah and the Books of Chronicles in relation to 1 and 2 Kings.

MATTHEW'S MOTIVES

The interesting question is: assuming that Matthew used Mark as the basic framework for his own writing and had it before him as he wrote, what was going through his mind as he went about the work? Or: why did he find Mark sufficiently unsatisfactory to make him undertake the task all over again? Why not rest content? It was not, after all, as if it was the fashionable thing to do (though probably the small numbers of literate Christians at the time made that in any case unlikely). A number of scenarios present themselves.

Convenience

There might have been a forceful argument of sheer convenience. Matthew's plain interest in the useful and the practical speaks in its favour. We saw that the 'grasping' of Mark works best when it is heard in a single session. His intricacies of theme and wording are lost when he comes before us in bits. But how practical was such a use? You could hear him every now and then, but not as often as you wished to hear something of the story of Jesus. It may be that Matthew wrote, at least in part, to meet such a need. The evidence lies in the signs that his book is marked so as to be divisible into seven sections (though other divisions are certainly possible but into longer and surely less practical parts):

chapters 1—2;
chapters 3—7;
8.1—11.1;
11.2—13.53;
13.54—19.2;
19.3—26.1;
26.2—28.20.

The clue is the mark of 'punctuation' given by the (admittedly not identical but still easily recognizable) formula that ends the five major sections of discourse, noting that Jesus had now 'finished these sayings'. To these five divisions we add the prefatory stories of Jesus' origins and the concluding stories of his passion and resurrection. Of course, if these divisions served their purpose at the beginning, that did not endure: they were still too long. But we can see that they would have served well for Matthew's clear instructional purposes. It is a schoolmaster's (old-style) way of providing for his pupils. Moreover, we have seen that Matthew failed to perceive some of Mark's subtleties of wording (e.g. the use of 'split' in both 1.10 and 15.38), perhaps a sign that he did not feel bound to hold on to the reception of the book as a single whole.

A scribe for the kingdom

If we set Matthew in the context of his world, a quite different possibility emerges. There is every sign that he had the training of a Jewish scribe: he handles scriptural passages with ease and skill, using the interpretative methods of his day. Moreover, it is common to read his reference to 'a scribe "discipled" for the kingdom of heaven' (13.52) as the author's semi-concealed signature (not to mention his – unique – reference to Christian scribes at 23.34, our only sign that such persons existed). If Matthew was good at interpreting texts and keen to use his skill in his new Christian cause, it is no wonder that he felt the need to improve on Mark, the story of Jesus that had come his way. He had, let us say, had Mark for ten years, and it was now time to bring out its 'true' meaning with a new kind of precision. His expounding, often with great ingenuity and skill, of texts from the old Scriptures backs up every major feature of Jesus' life and work, thus showing that he was indeed God's Messiah. For example, his parabolic teaching is backed in principle by the quoting of Psalm 78.2 at Matthew 13.35, and his healing by the use of Isaiah 53.4 at 8.17. This would both bolster faith and give ammunition for controversy with neighbouring Jews who had not converted.

It was time too to answer people's legitimate questions – questions that Mark had conspicuously failed to answer or had left hanging in the air. For example, what then happened after the strange position recorded in Mark 16.8? Jesus 'came from Nazareth' (1.9) as an adult, but what were the circumstances of his birth? Judas 'handed over' his Master; so what happened to him (see 27.3–10, and all is clear)? Matthew answers all these questions. Putting it another way: Mark 1.1 was filled out by Matthew 1.18–25, with its prominent key scriptural quotations; Mark 12.35–37 (Jesus as both 'son' and 'lord' of David) is explained and proved by the genealogy in Matthew 1.1–17.

The more we focus on these matters (Matthew's provision of scriptural backing and of answers to questions left in the air by Mark) the more we are likely to see him as a beneficent if unperceptive follower of his predecessor. He was, we might say, only trying to help. True, he missed a number of Mark's imaginative strokes, but he was a loyal and well-meaning player in the same team, and there would be many readers or hearers who would benefit from his helpful explanations and fillings-out. Of course, we know that well-meaning interpreters always intrude and are bound to falsify: the original writer, after all, meant to put matters in the way that he had chosen. Even translators cannot but falsify to some degree in moving from one tongue to another, even if they refrain from anything as crude as expressing opinions of their own where they disagree with the original.

Some of Matthew's alterations and additions to Mark are examples of such harmless self-revelation. For instance, it looks as if he could not stomach what he saw as Mark's crudities in telling of Jesus' mighty deeds. So the story of the cliff-plunging swine, filling 20 verses in Mark (5.1–20), shrinks to a mere seven (Matt. 8.28–34); and the story of the deaf mute at Mark 7.31–37, where Jesus uses crude techniques to effect a healing, is one of the very few passages that Matthew drops. There are signs of Matthew's fastidiousness or sense of propriety extending to a sense of social position. Not only is Jesus 'worshipped' frequently in Matthew (ten times, as opposed to twice in Mark, including once in mockery, 15.19), but those who reverence him include the astrologers (2.1–11), high-grade intellectuals in Matthew's world and so quite a catch, as they recognize their superior.

It may be that his skill was exercised with even greater (but still beneficent) originality. Goulder (1974) sought to show that Matthew had no substantial source beyond Mark, whose every detail he used to contribute to the composition of his own work, expanding and interpreting as he went. The theory has not won general agreement, but at least some aspects of it seem not improbable. For example, the Lord's Prayer (Matt. 6.9–13) can be seen as constructed from Marcan ingredients: the addressing of God as 'Father' and the prayer for forgiveness as one also forgives, together with the petitions for God's will to be done and to be spared the testing ('temptation'), look to Mark 11.25 and 14.32–42 (the former being omitted by Matthew in its place at 18.22). Matthew's pedagogic concern saw the need to provide explicitly for others what was implicit in Mark's depiction of Jesus. Christians must pray as Jesus had prayed.

All these moves are compatible with our seeing Matthew as the friendly interpreter and purveyor of Mark, making him easier to understand and more useful to developing Christian communities.

Points of disagreement

There are, however, signs that Matthew also had motives of another kind: he disagreed with Mark on important matters of faith and presentation, and was determined to protect Christian people from his influence. That he did not simply discard Mark and start again on a different basis would then be at first sight surprising – especially when we are aware of the extent of his disagreement. Perhaps we must conclude that material about Jesus was not as plentiful as we may suppose. Anyone who accepts Goulder's picture is of course bound to believe this; and it means that (contrary to academic orthodoxy) there was no collection of Jesus' sayings and other teaching available for Matthew's – and later Luke's – use. But even without such acceptance, we are likely to be surprised that he stuck to Mark as much as he plainly did, making him the basis of his own book.

So perhaps we should imagine another scenario. Matthew's church had received Mark and used it appreciatively for perhaps a decade. It would have been difficult for even a leader such as we may suppose Matthew to have been simply to bring its use to an end. Even if he had had the resources (and perhaps they could have been found) to make his own book from scratch, it would have been pastorally disastrous to end the use of the known and loved Gospel of Mark. One might, however, 'sell' the idea of amplifying it – and in the process make subtle alterations that rendered it acceptable, as well as adding material which gave a quite different thrust to the whole.

We may consider a modern parochial parallel. A new parish priest wishes to introduce a new hymn-book. His congregation resists: they fear the loss of old favourites. So a new book is found that includes most of those well-loved hymns but also many more new ones. The new book may also contain omissions from old hymns and subtle alterations to their wording that convey a different message, one which the new priest is keen to communicate. Moreover, in time, one might find that the selection of the old hymns became rarer and the new dominated the scene and (the priest hoped) formed the devotion of the people along sounder lines.

One may even imagine an example. It has become common in modern collections of hymns to omit from Mrs Alexander's popular hymn, 'All things bright and beautiful', a verse that has come to seem seriously dated:

> The rich man in his castle,
> The poor man at his gate,
> God made them, high or lowly,
> And ordered their estate.

Matthew was capable of comparable omissions; for example, he dropped Jesus' expansive saying at Mark 9.40: 'he that is not against us is for us'. Matthew was unhappy with such inclusiveness and had a more restrictive or disciplined sense of the Church. So not only did he omit this verse, but he included, in a different context, its precise opposite: 'He who is not with me is against me' (12.30). One might imagine modern hymn-book editors venturing to substitute in Mrs Alexander's hymn:

> The rich man in his castle,
> The poor man at his gate,
> God made them to be equal,
> And shared out the estate.

One may ask oneself how many in a modern congregation would notice what they had been led to sing and find their social attitudes thereby subtly altered; and how many in Matthew's community noticed that their sense of the Church was being radically changed.

MATTHEW'S OWN TEACHING

On what matters then did Matthew think Mark sufficiently misled and misleading that he was moved to write a second Gospel?

Minor corrections

There are small matters on which he has corrected Mark, where the motive seems to have been to smooth over possible disrespect to Jesus or others. They are commonly quoted as the best evidence that Mark was primary and Matthew his improver; for nobody would be likely (so it is argued) to make changes the other way round.

Mark 6.5

Jesus is rejected at Nazareth and 'he could do no mighty work there, except that he laid his hands upon a few sick people and healed them. And he marveled because of their unbelief.' The 'could' was not to be tolerated – the Messiah can do as he pleases. Hence: 'he did not do many mighty works there, because of their unbelief' (Matt. 13.58).

Mark 10.17

'"Good teacher, what must I do to inherit eternal life?" And Jesus said to him, "Why do you call me good? No one is good but God alone."' Here was an exploitable fault whereby Jesus could seem to be less than 'good'. So Matthew 19.16: '"Teacher, what good deed must I do, to have eternal life?" And he said to him, "Why do you ask me about what is good? One there is who is good."' The passage is surely still not immune to difficulty, but at least Matthew has 'improved' it; he is often a cautious corrector.

The Law

More serious is Matthew's thorough correction of passages where he saw Mark as cavalier with regard to the Jewish Law and its continuing validity under the regime of Jesus. We saw in the previous chapter numerous signs of Mark's having imbibed many of the essential perspectives of Paul. Especially where they mean a rejecting or marginalizing of the Law, and so the driving of a wedge between Judaism and the following of Jesus, Matthew is scrupulous at removing evidence of them. Thus Mark 7.19, cancelling the Jewish dietary rules, is simply omitted (and the passage given a different sense). Their non-application to gentile converts was at the heart of Paul's agenda and had been central to his quarrel with Peter (Gal. 2.11ff.). Luke places their removal at the mission of Peter to Cornelius (Acts 10—11) and the friendly settling of the issue at the Jerusalem meeting described in Acts 15. Common sense may lead to the view that Jesus would hardly have come up against the problem, and the probability is that Paul was the clear-eyed innovator and Mark was his evangelist; while Matthew, Jewish Christian, was an advocate of continuity (cf. Jesus' solid genealogy as the ground of his role, long before the baptism with which Mark announces his originality, like a bolt from the blue).

Similarly, Jesus' apparent relativizing of the sacrificial law at Mark 12.28–34 is strongly amended at Matthew 22.34–40, and it is made plain that the commands to love God and neighbour in no way reduce the force of 'all the law and the prophets'. We can see how recently the stark contrast between the two evangelists here has come to seem plain, in the putting together of Mark's 'there is no other commandment greater than these' with Matthew's 'on these two commandments hang all the law and the prophets' in the so-called 'summary of the law' in Anglican liturgies from 1928 on; and it remains unto this day, despite the fact that the second was written to obliterate the first! It does not, however, mean that Anglicans keep the whole Jewish Law.

But Matthew's Christians did; as 5.17–19 and 23.3, 23 show. The puzzle then is why this Gospel so speedily became top dog, always, it would seem, widely misunderstood on this issue, as ever since, by Christians who have no intention of obeying the Torah in its completeness; but, lacking the clear-sightedness of Paul and respecting the name of Matthew and welcoming so much of the clear teaching of Jesus which he records, they have read him for his backing of firm moral teaching, as well as the disciplinary system (Matt. 18) and prospect of seemingly fair graded judgement (16.27, 25), in which Matthew has been followed by secular and ecclesiastical authorities down the ages. It is true that Paul himself does not entirely lack similar sentiments (e.g. 2 Cor. 5.10), but Matthew has not grasped the force of the doctrine of the human situation found in (e.g.) Romans 3.23, which we found echoed in Mark. Not that Matthew is without a sense of Christ's graciousness, as 11.28–30 shows; but it is overlaid.

To see how Matthew's sense of Jesus as interpreter of the Law (as Messiah and so authoritative, yet he argues his case) is depicted, we need only mention Matthew's amending of Mark's sabbath-marginalizing passages, 2.23—3.6. In 12.1–14, he has shifted their tone from one of the subordinating of the sabbath to human need, even when not urgent, to one of casuistic argument, scripturally based, and limited to the matter in hand. The kingdom of God is a matter of detailed and just provisions rather than the majestic sweep of God's righteous rule (see Houlden, 1992, pp. 47–52).

The disciples

Whatever he perceived or failed to perceive of Mark's methods and rhetorical power, Matthew was not ready to retain the adverse picture of the disciples. It is not, however, that he was so cavalier with the story he had inherited that, for example, he rewrote the Passion to turn the disciples into heroes (as we shall see, Luke took steps in that direction); but he did seize every other opportunity to improve the wretched image that Mark gave to them. Where Mark says they did not understand (8.21), Matthew says that they did (16.12); the incomprehension of Mark 6.52 disappears in the scene of worship in the boat (14.33), where, as elsewhere, the disciples' worst fault is to be lacking in faith; that is to say that, like us all, they could do better, but were by no means condemned or ground into the dust. Similarly, though Matthew (unlike Luke) retains the calling of Peter 'Satan' (16.23), its force is reduced to almost ritual dimensions by the interposing of the encomium on Peter and his commissioning as prime apostle (16.17–19). And Peter's blunt rejection of Jesus' foretelling of his death (Mark 8.32) is made into a courtier's demurral (16.22).

Matthew's sense of justice according to deserts combines with his rescuing of the disciples in the treatment of Judas (27.3–10), who is in effect the scapegoat for the rest. Their restoration and promotion to the topmost place in the Christian mission is made plain in 28.16–20, just as their ultimate central role was bestowed at 19.28. It is no wonder that the improper request for special rewards voiced by James and John at Mark 10.35 is transferred by Matthew (20.20) to their mother, in a pardonable expression of pride. All the same, the reward is theirs: in that passage, he keeps some of Mark's negativity (20.24–28), but apostolic power is sure.

There can be no clearer evidence of the revolution in the understanding of the Gospels in recent years than the recognition that so many of these matters of comparison, now seeming so clear in their likely implications, have gone unremarked for so long;

and even when remarked, their far-reaching significance was not pursued. Earlier, attention was drawn to Irenaeus' embryonic sense of the 'flavours' of the different Gospels. One is bound to feel that his perception of the various qualities of the four is very different from the theological emphases and religious concerns that now strike us. What now seems so obvious to us was then wholly opaque. We trust that we are closer to discerning some of the perceptions held by first-century Christians and some of the pressures under which they followed out their calling. Matthew, it seems, not only failed to grasp Mark's subtlety but also was aware of needs in the Church (for direction, clarity and order) which were less prominent for Mark. Perhaps the passing of a decade or so had been crucial (see Richardson (ed.), 1953, pp. 382f.).

This wide-ranging discussion has sought to identify Matthew's motives in both using and yet altering the Gospel of Mark so drastically. By a mixture of evidence on the page, of which we make sense with varying degrees of confidence, and hypothesis, we have built up a picture of his mind that does not lack coherence; though even then, there is a puzzling mixture in Matthew of faithful respect for Mark and disagreement with some of the chief features of his message. We suggested (in the hymn-book parallel) that perhaps he found himself driven to a measure of pastoral guile; if that is correct, he was presumably one of the first Christian pastors to proceed in that way. He was certainly not the last.

But, despite his clear disagreements with Mark on a number of central matters, he was nevertheless happy to do what he surely saw as clarifying Mark and firming up some of his hints. Such firmness is indeed one of Matthew's leading characteristics: like many Christian leaders after him, he is all for definiteness. We may suppose that, though this was no doubt in part a matter of temperament, it may also have been a matter of pastoral necessity. As the first century proceeded, churches were more and more in need of firm guidance and of rulings on a number of matters. Most obviously applying to Matthew's rather than Jesus' day, we can point to the material in 18.15–20 about the settling of disciplinary cases, and perhaps the guidance on prayer, almsgiving and fasting in chapter 6, the pious duties of a Christian (as indeed of a Jew).

The guidance on prayer, as we saw, illustrates his readiness to develop Mark and make much of what was present there only in embryo. Thus, though Mark uses the term 'son' for Jesus' relation to God a few times (e.g. 1.11; 3.11; 14.62; 15.39), only twice is God referred to as 'father' (11.25; 14.36). We suggested that this could be the root of Matthew's version of the Lord's Prayer; but it may be the root of much else besides, for Matthew is dedicated to the sense of God as 'my', 'our', 'your' father and it appears at every turn (e.g. 5.16, 45, 48; 6.1, 4, 6, 14, 15, 18 – to go no further). This leading feature of Matthew's belief about God occurs both in passages that are his own (whether derived from other sources or not) and in others where he has adapted Mark. For an example of the latter, in the Last Supper scene, Mark's prophecy concerning the cup, of the day when Jesus will 'drink it new in the kingdom of God' (14.25) becomes 'drink it new with you in my Father's kingdom' (26.29). As we saw, it is hard not to see here a case of Matthew fastening on to a theme that appears in embryo in Mark, finding it congenial, and making much of it. What is interesting about this feature is that it moves in a different direction from that which seems to explain many of Matthew's developments, i.e. the need to fortify the sense of ethical definiteness and to provide instructional backbone for a developing church. It does however certainly tell us much about Matthew's theological priorities: here too, he is far from uninterested.

Loosely, Mark was a work of profound theological insight, but it took a certain kind of understanding to grasp his subtleties. We may say that they tend to have the character of poetry. Matthew had been to a different school and partly missed Mark's points, because he had not grasped his mode of writing, and partly had other priorities, other schemes to develop, and worked with a kind of Jewish prose that served those purposes; so his using of Mark includes cases that look sometimes obtuse, sometimes simply understandable developments, sometimes deliberate rejections of Marcan doctrine (as most notably in his attitude to the Jewish Law's continuing validity for Christians and in his sense of the disciples as the more or less exemplary leaders of the Church, to be looked back on with admiration).

MATTHEW AT WORK

We have been concerned with Matthew's motivation. Let us move to another level and ask what precisely he saw as the plan of his book; or else, what scheme would he use that both incorporated most of Mark (in adapted form) and yet offered something that was unmistakably new? The plain man's view, that he simply had more information to put down than Mark had, is surely not a sufficient answer. Rising above that unhelpful simplicity, we can say, at the very least, that Matthew thought he should attend to both the beginning and the end of the book; and, as we saw, this was primarily in order to answer questions left hanging in the air by the earlier evangelist – that is, as Matthew looked at the matter (even though it probably meant he had mistaken and underestimated Mark's purpose).

So, first, the question of Jesus' origins. Mark had, almost in parentheses, told us something of them: he came from Nazareth (6.1–6), and he had a mother and brothers (and perhaps sisters, but manuscripts differ) (3.31–35). But these things are included, not, it seems, out of possible biographical interest, but, as was suggested above, in order to show how certain groups were consistently opposed or indifferent to Jesus. In other words, this information is not given at all in order to answer a question concerning Jesus' antecedents. That it does so, in its own off-hand way, is almost incidental. What matters is that Jesus is rejected by those who might have supported him, or rather, that as God's anointed one, he is alone in the face of all. It is therefore a theological point, not a historical or genealogical one. It helps us to see better who Jesus is; that it refers to Jesus' family is wholly secondary, even, almost, a matter of chance. In any case, God's chosen servants had rarely met support from their close families: aloneness went with the vocation.

In contrast, by Matthew's time (or, more strictly, for Matthew the evangelist), the question of Jesus' origins has become a matter of importance. What were those origins? Were they the correct origins for the Messiah? Did he measure up to the specifications? Perhaps this was to answer a developing agenda among thoughtful

Christians; perhaps in order to answer interested or scornful Jews who thought the Christians' beliefs about Jesus erroneous, even infamous. Whatever the precise motivation, Matthew provided a full answer to the questions as a powerful preface to the book he had inherited. That preface could make Mark's opening (now in Matt. 3) seem pale. It became subordinate, simply the first episode of Jesus' ministry whose credentials had been settled at the time of his birth; his baptism was simply the opening, sponsored by God, of his active ministry.

Matthew's full answer was in a form that would surely impress, even silence, objecting Jews. At the least, the argument was set out in powerful terms. The genealogy established Jesus' pedigree as messianic; and the subsequent story of the preliminaries to his birth and then the event and its impressive aftermath, with the visit of the magi, plus his Moses-like sojourn in Egypt, were set out as the fulfilment of prophecy, the true meaning of a series of important texts, whose secret was now at last disclosed. Here, the author shows himself to be a skilled operator in the matter of scribal techniques (as the near-contemporary Dead Sea Scrolls demonstrate, using very similar methods, of course for their own different purposes). Goulder (1974) has even suggested that his setting out of 3 x 14 generations might be intended (following the fashionable date symbolism of the time) to point to its equivalent, 6 x 7, each of the six representing a 'day' in the process of history, so that Jesus' coming was a kind of sabbath, a day of fulfilment, with his resurrection signifying day eight, the start of the new dispensation. Certainly, one of Matthew's key original passages, 11.28–30, with its two uses of 'rest' as marking Jesus' purpose, makes clear reference to the meaning of sabbath. It really does seem that these two chapters carry important meaning for Matthew at a number of levels. In their own way, they leave Mark standing!

Matthew had to make a few adjustments to other parts of the Gospel as a result of his positive picture of Jesus' family, warranted by Scripture. So he omits Mark 3.21–22, where his family declare him mad, and softens Mark 3.31–35 (= Matt. 12.46–50) to make it less offensive and more a harmless illustration of what being a follower of Jesus is like. And if Matthew saw a Mary who is at the tomb ('mother of James and Joseph', 27.56; cf. 13.55) as Jesus' mother, this is less surprising, and there is nothing ambiguous about her behaviour (28.8–10).

So, as Matthew 'improved' the (to him) unsatisfactory opening of Mark, so he also improved the even more unsatisfactory ending. Again, questions are answered: how did the message get out? Answer: the women were not silent but told, and did it gladly. What do we say to the rumour that the disciples stole Jesus' body? Answer: there was a guard, so it would have been impossible, and they were bribed to keep quiet (27.62–66; 28.1–15). And did Jesus ever see his disciples in Galilee? Answer: certainly he did, and it was their commissioning to carry on his mission and his teaching with his full authority. The final section (28.16–20) is in fact a passage that is crammed with Matthew's key beliefs: Jesus as the one with God's authority, for always; the mission as a recruiting of pupils for the school of the Messiah, where his teaching (presumably, as recorded in Matthew's Gospel) would be handed on (v. 19). It is the Church's charter, until the end of the age. And if Mark's ending seemed (to the undiscerning eye) to be limp, there is no doubting the power of Matthew's substitute. For him, surely, Mark had simply not been good enough (or was it that Mark was too subtle, too allusive?).

The emphasis on teaching (rather than, for example, evangelizing or preaching or following) as the duty of the disciples, as set out in the final section (v. 19) takes us to Matthew's other chief structural innovation.

Matthew decided to make Jesus' teaching both orderly and prominent by organizing significant parts of it into coherent blocks of material, each focusing on a different aspect of Christian life or belief. As we saw, it was not that Mark had underplayed 'Jesus as teacher', but in Matthew's view he had provided far too little in the way of practical and useful guidance. We cannot tell exactly why this was: it may be simply that Mark's 'vision' worked chiefly in more theological or relational (and, we might say, spiritual) ways – what mattered was who Jesus was and how one could relate to him and his work. Matthew, however, while not underplaying those dimensions (even if he saw them differently), was aware of other needs: guidance on issues and the shape of ideals for Christian living. There may also be a generational factor. Though the gap between the writing of the two Gospels was not great, it may have been enough for at least some Christian communities to feel in need of more answers to more practical questions and some Christian leaders to feel moved to supply them. How he found the necessary material is disputed. We referred to the radical view that he found it in Mark, taking every advantage of hints found there and using them to satisfy his own new and different needs. The more usual view is, naturally, that there was a traditional body of Jesus' sayings that had been handed down, perhaps even written down, in the churches and was available to Matthew as a reservoir that would help to meet his needs. Let us assume that there was such a body of material which indeed he could have supplemented.

There can then be a range of views about the degree of adaptation that Matthew felt free to use in order to make the material serve his own purposes. The most common scholarly belief is that he shared such a body of (probably written?) material with Luke (it is referred to as Q – for German *Quelle*, 'source'), and that for the most part Luke was more inclined to reproduce it in its 'original' form. There can be all kinds of belief (really, no firm evidence) on the relation of this material to what Jesus actually taught, though connections there must be. On any showing, it is fragmentary, isolated from its original context, and of course from other vital matters like tone of voice, look of face. Moreover, while Luke's version may often look (hunch?) more original, it also now tends to be seen as more Lucan, the Lucan way of thinking and writing being something we now feel more able than in earlier days to define and recognize. In any case, Matthew's version of many of these shared sayings appears to have gone through the creative agency of his own mind, in the same way that Mark did: it bears his stamp. In many ways, the two 'sources' cohere – as we should expect of a rational author. (We discussed the example of Matthew's use of 'father' for God.)

The five discourses

But our chief concern here is with his forming of five discourses out of Jesus' teaching material, apparently with the aim of providing an orderly and usable compendium, though within the narrative context of the Gospel as a whole. (We can contrast the not un-Matthean – in terms of content – collection made up exclusively of teaching, the *Didache*, dating, probably, from not very much later; see Louth (ed.), 1987.)

The five discourses differ in the degree of their reliance on Mark (mostly in the third and fifth), as well as in theme. They are identifiable not only by their kind of subject matter but also by their almost-standard ending, to the effect that Jesus had ended 'these sayings'. We should also note that there are occasional passages of teaching in Mark which Matthew has incorporated in their place, without reference to the five main blocks, e.g. Matthew 15.1–21; cf. Mark 7.1–23. The five blocks are as follows:

1 5—7: 'the Sermon on the Mount'. It is the most general of the five, giving basic guidance to the spirit and character of Christian life as enjoined by Jesus; including Matthew's insistence on the Jewish Law as the basis for Christians which they must retain and observe (5.17–19; cf. 23.3, 23), but at an intensified level, amounting to 'perfection' (5.20–48). It is worked out in the duties of almsgiving, prayer and fasting, to be fulfilled in a spirit of unself-concerned and single-minded devotion. In the final passage, 7.13–end, the need to remain loyal to the whole teaching of Jesus, including the Jewish Law which it subsumes, is further emphasized: and the lesser, if enthusiastic, obedience of some Christians is curtly dismissed (7.21–23).

2 10.5—11.1: instructions for Christian missionaries. This speech is designed for itinerant Christians, as distinct from those who live in settled communities or congregations (see chapter 18). In that way, the forms of Christian life known to Matthew are not unlike those of the Essenes, who also had bodies of rules for different styles of observance. A notable feature of this collection of instructions is Matthew's decision to transfer to this setting material which Mark had included in his chapter 13, the prophecy of what would happen at the End. Mark saw this as a time when the faithful could reckon to suffer persecution by authorities, both Jewish and Roman or Herodian, and indeed by family members. Matthew sees such persecution as part of the daily fare of Christian missionaries, here and now (vv. 17–22; cf. Mark 13.9–13).

3 13.1–53: parables. This chapter is in a sense a reflective pause in the sequence of teaching blocks, for it includes, on a Marcan base (chiefly the story of the sower, vv. 1–23), a collection of parables, some of which look back to chapter 10, with encouragement for Christian evangelism (those on the treasure and the pearl, vv. 44–45, as indeed the sower itself), while others are concerned with church discipline and so look ahead to chapter 18 (tares and dragnet, vv. 24–30, 36–43, 47–50).

4 18.1—19.1: the discipline of Christian congregations. Matthew sets out practical rules (very like those of the Essenes). They are both 'enlightened' (forgiveness must be generous and free) and (to the modern eye) fierce, for there is to be no indulgence of the slipshod (18.15–35). They are therefore designed to promote order and discipline on the one hand and brotherly harmony on the other. 'Brotherly'? And sisterly, almost certainly, but surely subordinately. Like Mark (and unlike Luke), Matthew does not include wives among those whom Jesus' followers are to forsake (19.29), though he does provide for their dismissal in certain circumstances (19.9; cf. 5.32). This provision for one-way divorce (i.e. wives have no such power) may testify once more to Matthew's more firmly communal perspective, with the resulting human problems requiring resolution. And he acknowledges the place of celibate members, 19.12 (again as at Qumran). 'Wandering' members (morally or in seeking to leave the community?) are to be brought back: loyalty is therefore reciprocal and pastoral care is most resolutely given (18.12–14).

5 24.3—26.1: we have already found that though Matthew shows structural purpose in providing five discourses (with possible Mosaic and Pentateuchal overtones), he has not included all his teaching material within their bounds. Here, for example, chapter 23 is the climax of his anti-Pharisaic case, reflecting surely the intensity of local internecine strife (for Matthew is both like them, v. 3, and – therefore? – fiercely opposed to them). The formal discourses are set apart by their thematic distinctiveness, in this final case teaching concerning the coming End. Like the third discourse (Matt. 13), it is built on a Marcan foundation (Mark 13). It is extended chiefly by means of parables which are further evidence

of Matthew's definiteness: there must be no mistaking the need for vigilance, which Mark enjoined briefly, 13.32–37, and which, perhaps on the basis of ingredients in that passage, Matthew now emphasizes in some of his more terrifying teaching (e.g. 25.12–13; 29–30). In 25.31–46, he faces the obvious question: what will be the basis for dealing with the non-Christian bulk of the human race? The narrowness of what is probably the gist of his solution gives the impression that he has scarcely got the measure of the task's magnitude! Though the traditional interpretation certainly survives (that acts of charity will be the yardstick), comparison with 10.40–42 points to the view that Matthew sees generosity to Christian missionaries as the basis for judgement. His sense of the world and of the human race is surely bounded by very local horizons. Matthew (unlike Luke) was no traveller.

But Matthew is not all judgement and vengeance (cf. 16.27). In a passage that does not come from Mark and receives prominence almost at the centre of the book, we have a passage that is among the most sublime statements of Jesus' beneficent ministry as Messiah (11.28–30). It is a mission of generosity and mercy: 'For my yoke is easy and my burden is light.' In the light of the teaching discourses, that can only be true if one knows and rejoices in the personal lordship of Jesus. We should note the prominence in Matthew of the adjective 'meek' (5.5; 11.29; 21.5; cf. 12.18–21). Far from being a 'weak' word, it was seen as a prime characteristic of the ideal and strong king, who would refrain from bombast and arrogance (see Good, 1999).

There is no stronger evidence of Matthew's outlook and its differences from Mark than in the passion narrative. At first sight he follows Mark closely, but his changes are deliberate and important. All of them make for answering outstanding questions, left in the air by Mark (at least to the eye of enquirers like Matthew or his people), and for tying up loose ends. So: what happened to Judas? He met his just deserts, and in that way (for Matthew, not Mark) he differed from the rest of the Twelve (28.16–20). Could Jesus have escaped? Of course he could, but valiantly, and with meekness, he faced his necessary fate (26.53). Was he really abandoned by God? No, heaven made itself plain at the time (27.51–54; 28.2–4). Was Pilate (= Rome) really against him? No, only out of fear (27.19, 24), and the responsibility lay wholly with the Jews (27.25). Especially in the last case, clarity was bought at a terrible cost (see Houlden, 1987).

Matthew expressed his theology in terms of story, as did Mark. We have seen that he did it in his own different way, but using the same basic method. They agreed that narrative was the way to make faith plain, but varied in priorities and perspectives. But it is easy to see why, quite apart from the attaching of the apostolic name, Matthew was found the more 'useful' of the two. Was he not more 'one of us'?

4

Luke: Man of Jesus and Man of the World

The realism of a secular gospel is Luke's grand achievement.
(Drury, 1976, p. 180)

Mark told of Jesus as if he were a bolt from the blue: yes, some prophecy from the past; yes, a future somehow, somewhere; but it was the present that counted, and if you read Mark, you lived again in Jesus' present, fused with your own. Matthew was more cautious, more conscious of his Jewish tradition and of a public to persuade as well as a church to manage. So he 'placed' Jesus: he came from a known Jewish heritage and was now in heaven as lord of the world. To be a Christian was to live in that assured and, to that degree, comfortable setting, come what may.

Luke went a step further. As his opening four verses show, he did it deliberately. Like Matthew, he was not content with what was already on offer. He went further because of his own formation and his place in the world. In a way, Matthew had done the same; but Luke's world was bigger and he observed it with keen eyes. How big his world was, in terms of knowledge from experience, it is not possible to say exactly, though, despite doubts, there is still something to be said for the plain reader's view that he had accompanied Paul in some of his travels (yet it is undeniable that he had not absorbed very much of Paul's favourite vocabulary or mode of thought): see the so-called 'we' passages in the second half of Acts. More important, he shows knowledge of the geography, and of the life and government of some of the cities of the eastern Mediterranean world and feels at home in describing them. (Though some of his knowledge is what might be hearsay – it is tourists' stuff – clever men at Athens and silversmiths for the cult of Artemis at Ephesus: it is as if Paul visits London and goes to the changing of the guard and to Paris and visits the Eiffel Tower.) Whether he knew the land of Jesus' life first-hand is more doubtful. His geography of Palestine is not always intelligible and he seems to see the Jerusalem temple as able to serve as a kind of lecture theatre for visiting speakers (Luke 19.47—20.1), like corresponding locations in Paul's career.

We can sum up thus: Luke was pictorially minded, interested in the world around him, including places and persons. So his scenario tends to be more exciting (and indeed frequently more cheerful) than that of his fellow-evangelists. What is more, he can be described not only as the first Christian travel-writer but, perhaps more grandly, as the first Christian historian. Matthew might deserve that title, for, as we saw, he certainly has a sense of the past, but it is a Jewish scribe's interest in history, fixing Jesus' pedigree, rather than anything wider or more human. Luke is also interested in Jesus' pedigree but he traces it back beyond Abraham (as Matthew) to Adam (3.23–38), father of the human race, and places Jesus in the human world of rulers and times and places (2.1; 3.1–2). Whether he always does it accurately is secondary to his setting out to do it at all. For a person of his station in life to get these things exactly right in the world of his time would be a major achievement: where could one turn for records and agreed dates?

At the same time, he is a Christian with a strong scriptural formation and a theological perspective. It is a combination of qualities which makes Luke unique in early Christianity. He is then no mere chronicler, putting down one thing after another as information has come his way. As we shall see, he has arrived at an intellectual pattern according to which he views the past and the world. Usefully, he began his Gospel with a statement of intention. It is somewhat surprising (though not to those who know the tradition of his secular profession) that his stylish preface (the best Greek of the book) appears to be written after the model, not of histories but of medical (and surely other) text-books (see Alexander, 1993). So Paul's Luke, 'the beloved physician' (Col. 4.14), remains the most likely of the four evangelists to be the person traditionally said to be a Gospel's author; though he was in any case a good candidate for the eirenical and unifying purposes of the second century when the identifications were made – a friend of Paul and in his writing an approver of Peter.

Was not such a man a rare bird? A man of the gentile world, with some education to his credit, yet using – and comfortable with – the Jewish Scriptures and devoted to the decisive role in God's purposes of Jesus the Jew and then to the work of Jesus' followers, especially Peter and Paul. How could such a one come about? In his writing, he includes a number of characters who are perhaps people after his own heart: gentiles who are friends and associates of Judaism. In the Gospel itself, there is the centurion who 'loves our nation and built us our synagogue' (7.5); and in Acts there are numerous people who are attached to Judaism, concealed by innocuous English expressions: they were 'devout' or 'feared God' (Cornelius, 10.1), or they were 'worshippers of God', like Lydia (16.14). Such persons belonged to the recognized category of 'God-fearers', gentiles who had associated them-selves with Judaism, attracted by its combination of venerability, prayer and study, so offering a religious combination that was scarcely available in conventional paganism, with its sacrificial ceremonies, or even, in the same deeply learned way, in mystery cults. It was of course more demanding to convert to Judaism, and even then hard to achieve the 'belongingness' of the born Jew. It is likely that Christianity, as presented by Paul and his associates, was attractive to such people, offering full membership to Jews and gentiles, men and women alike (Gal. 3.26–28). And it is not improbable that Luke our author was of their number: he has a feeling for them and he shares all their interests. (See on Mark, p. 28.)

But what did he think of those who had already attempted the task which he set himself? His preface tells us that 'many' had been there before him. Mark and the 'sayings source' (Q) that perhaps he shares with Matthew? But then Q is not a Gospel, not an attempt at the task which Luke now undertakes. So perhaps Mark and Matthew? But had there already been others that have disappeared, and could he mean the Gospel of John? The idea that John preceded Luke has had a few advo-cates, and certainly there are some links between them alone (e.g. Martha and Mary, Luke 10.38–42 and John 11), though of vanished Gospels we can say nothing. That Luke knew and used Matthew as well as Mark has a number of distinguished advocates (most powerfully Goulder, 1989). Notice: the more

one thinks of evangelists as men with minds and ideas, the more
possible it is for them to use sources in surprisingly creative
ways; whereas, if they were merely dovetailing sources in an
operation of humdrum literary fusion, it remains less likely that
Luke used both Mark and Matthew alone – too much of
Matthew is left out. On any showing, it was a tour de force. For
our purpose, this is in any case a secondary matter, for our
concern is to grasp his intent from the finished product, and to
understand how his faith is expressed in his story. Perhaps
Luke's 'many' was always a harmless exaggeration.

ONE IDEA OR TWO?

A more pressing question for the reader who wishes to get hold
of Luke's 'mind' as an evangelist concerns the connection
between the Gospel and the Acts of the Apostles. Despite their
centuries-long separation in the New Testament, there is no
serious doubt that the two are the work of the same author or
that, in some way, Acts is the Gospel's sequel (Acts 1.1).
Sequels, however, are not all of the same kind. Sometimes a
writer (or a film-maker) produces a first work which receives
such a favourable (and profitable) reception that he is persuaded
or determined to make a second. Or else he plans a two-part
work from the start. The ending of Luke's Gospel may be taken
to favour the former view of this case. It speaks of Christ's
departure by ascending to heaven, and, as we shall see, the final
reference to the apostles' joy and visit to the temple is thoroughly typical of Luke. It could not be a better conclusion. Acts
then begins by recapitulating the story of the ascension, using
it as its introduction. But it may be better to see the departure
at the end of Luke 24 as referring simply to the end of Easter
Day. Acts 1.1–3 then tells of Jesus' numerous comings and
goings for 40 days, until his final departure described in vv. 6–
11. In that case, we may – and perhaps should – read the Gospel
and Acts as a two-part work, planned as a single whole according to a single vision of things. If so, Luke has acted with a quite
new degree of originality, producing a fresh idea of what is
important about Jesus and his story, and the mission is part and
parcel with the life. In that case, certainly, if we are to grasp his

purpose, we must attend to the work as a whole. Are there signs that this is the right way to think?

- There are close parallels between deeds of Jesus and deeds of apostles: e.g. the raising of Jairus' daughter (Luke 8.40–56) and that of Tabitha (Acts 9.36–43); Jesus' feedings of crowds (e.g. Luke 9.10–17) and Paul's feeding of an equally 'unconverted' group on the ship after the storm in Acts 27.

- There are items omitted from the Gospel but included in Acts: e.g. the threat against the temple does not appear in the trial of Jesus in Luke 22 but does appear in the trial of Stephen, Acts 6.13. The 'cleansing of foods' in Mark 7 (cf. v. 19) is dropped, but the point is achieved, not by Jesus but by Peter as a result of a vision in Acts 10—11.

- There is a doctrine that the apostle is as his master. So the sufferings of Stephen, Peter and Paul are, in varying ways, reminiscent of those of Jesus. The first is the most obvious case, with Stephen's final words in Acts 7.59–60 reminding us of Jesus' words from the cross at Luke 23.34 and 46. But Peter's temporary imprisonment in Acts 12 also has features reminiscent of Jesus' passion: it happens at passover; he is placed between two guards, as was Jesus between two thieves; he is 'raised' miraculously; and on arriving home is taken for an angel, as Jesus (in Luke alone, 24.39) was taken for a 'spirit'. The same is true of Paul's ultimate (or rather penultimate) endurance-test, the near-death experience at sea in Acts 27, where he holds a quasi-eucharistic meal (v. 35), whose aim is to provide 'salvation' (v. 34; Greek *soteria*; NRSV 'strength' misses the message). His open preaching in Rome may even be meant as a kind of resurrection, confirming his survival of the tomb-like seas (cf. Pss. 130; 69).

- The overarching activity of the Spirit binds the two volumes into a whole, dominating the first four chapters of the Gospel in particular and then taken up in Acts 2 at Pentecost; under whose aegis the entire mission is authorized and empowered.

THE SINGLE SWEEP

We must try to identify Luke's strategy as a whole. His picture of things is displayed in distinct dimensions.

Temporal

Luke sees time in three phases centring on the career of Jesus (see Conzelmann, 1960). This is the only phase that he describes in full and it is the centre of his picture of time. The previous phase, all that precedes Jesus, takes place off stage, but Luke's awareness of its importance is made plain in his telling of phase two. The story of the succeeding phase, the Church's mission until the End, is described in its opening episodes, in Acts, and its ultimate destiny is described in apocalyptic passages in the Gospel itself (chapters 17 and 21). So all is provided for, the historical picture is clear, but the three phases are treated differently.

Unlike Josephus, for example, Luke did not think it necessary to tell the whole biblical story again from the beginning. He covered it – in a number of ways. First, in speaking of Jesus as 'fulfilling' it: Luke 24.32, 44. So the risen Jesus at last gives the key to his life-story. Second, by way of the genealogy (3.23–38), which, like the Old Testament, takes the story back to the creation. It is, however, the creation of Adam, not of the world: Luke's world is people-centred, through and through. He is no environmentalist. And he traces the story back from Jesus, who is the centre, rather than forwards as Matthew did. In that way, Matthew follows the order of Scripture, while Luke prefers to move back from the middle of time, where Jesus is.

He covered phase one in a third, literary way: by writing the story of Jesus' birth (and surrounding events) in the style of the (Greek) old Scriptures. This Septuagintal style extends from language to people and themes. The Magnificat (Luke 1.46–55) virtually reproduces Hannah's song of praise at the birth of Samuel in 1 Samuel 2. The Nunc Dimittis (2.29–32) reminds us of Isaiah (52.10; 42.6; 49.6) and Simeon who speaks it makes us think of Eli (1 Sam. 1—2).

Jesus is embedded in the sacred past – and goes beyond it, but without rejecting it. So in 2.41–52, where the boy Jesus attends a kind of seminar in the temple with learned teachers of the Law, he both listens and asks questions. Notice that at this point (contrary to artists' depictions of the scene, unduly influenced by later Christian doctrine) Jesus does not himself teach: he receives what has gone before; though 'all who heard him were amazed at his understanding and his answers' (v. 47). He is a sort of prodigy, but his role at this stage of Luke's history is to receive from phase one and its representatives. His stepping on to the stage in his own right is still to come. At the same time, even phase three is already foreseen (as it had been in the Old Testament): Jesus is 'a light for revelation to the gentiles' (2.32). And the cross as the route to it is alluded to in 2.35. In this way, Luke 1—2, besides simply telling us the story of Jesus' antecedents (in a way that Mark had failed to do), and so answering our natural questions, makes a number of doctrinal points about God's purpose that is to be fulfilled through Jesus. And the passage does it as much by creating a certain ethos (we might describe it as sacred 'olde worlde') as by, implicitly, making points that could be translated into abstract terms. It is necessary for Luke's readers to absorb the ethos as well as the doctrine: perhaps not all his readers (many of them gentile Christians of the later first century) could see the point of so much emphasis on the old Jewish story and its books. In the most attractive way, Luke seduces them (and his readers ever since) into seeing that past as part of their own story. And every Christmas reinforces the point.

The reference to 'seduction' has particular force for modern readers. In Luke's world, both gentile and Jewish, the establishing of one's roots was a vital part of identity, as was living in the light of them. For most people (there were exceptions – the Athenian intelligentsia, Acts 17.21), novelty held no attraction, possessed no virtue. For modern Western readers, though the seduction still works, as the reference to Christmas was intended to show, it now appeals less to the head, less to people's sense of vital identity, defining our place in life, and becomes instead a matter of gloss and warm feelings, usually centred on the family, our remaining repository of ideals. It is not surprising that the culture of Christmas which brings that past before us has become so sentimental or magical, so ephemeral, so little connected, except in a clutching kind of hope, with 'real life'. It was not like that for Luke and his readers.

These chapters make a bridge between phase one and phase two. For the latter, Luke is dependent on Mark (and perhaps Matthew – certainly much other material, some of it also in Matthew). Mark provides his basic outline, but he is not afraid to deal with it 'creatively' (as so often, a euphemism for transformation), as 1.1–4 warns us. We shall turn later to the Gospel's mode of operation, and this is not the place to dwell on the actual working of Luke's second phase. But we note two significant and necessary innovations that he has introduced.

First, he finds in Mark 6.1–6 the story of Jesus' rejection at Nazareth and decides to bring it forward, making of it a policy-stating, paradigmatic episode that will shed its light over the whole of the rest of Jesus' ministry. So in 4.16–30 we have what is in effect Jesus' key-note speech, determining the thrust of his whole work as Luke sees it, followed by its polarizing effect. The 'speech' itself is in fact no such thing: like the ethos of chapters 1—2, this too is pure Scripture, not a sermon but a reading. His own single sentence, 'Today this scripture has been fulfilled in your hearing', is both brief and yet crucial (v. 21). Jesus' policy is itself nothing new; it is that envisaged by Isaiah in holy words (61.1–2; 58.6). Scripture too, this time in episodes recalled, puts on the table the necessity of gentile mission: God's saving purposes are for the good of all (4.24–27).

Second, in order to make way for the story that Acts will unfold, where Jesus' physical, visible presence is no longer available, it is necessary to remove him from the scene. As we saw, this is achieved first in the last verses of the Gospel; and they pave the way for the opening of Acts where the final ascension is described and the Spirit is unleashed with unprecedented force (though again foreseen in Scripture, Joel 2.28–32), compensating, as it were, for the absence of Jesus. There is no loss whatsoever of divine force in the world.

Luke's mode of telling these things may easily strike us (and would surely have struck some Christians of his time, for example the author of the Fourth Gospel) as having something of the crude staginess that we find in baroque opera, with gods ascending on wooden clouds and descending on wires. 'The Other' is (perforce it seems) physically located: it is an outcome, in Luke's own world, of his vivid sense of place and person and time. And it is part of what makes him now so readable.

The theme of the third phase is, however, the Christian mission that precedes the End and Christ's return. Luke might have chosen to take his story of the mission down to his own day, leaving open what would happen the day after he laid down his pen. But Acts is no mere chronicle, no simple agglomeration of items, without shape or message. Its general programme is stated in 1.8, with the message going from Jerusalem and Jewish circles to Samaria and then gentile lands ('the uttermost parts of the earth'), with Rome, it seems, as their climactic symbol. The spaciousness of the final category is narrowed, naturally, to the world of Luke's knowledge, the lands bordering the Eastern Mediterranean on its eastern and northern sides, and, in effect, chiefly to the missions of Paul, who is, in ways which we cannot fully define, Luke's hero and master.

There are, however, other aspects of phase three which, like the first two, should affect the way we read the Gospel. Luke is greatly concerned to stress the essential unity of the mission, even flying in the face of what we know, chiefly from Galatians 1—2 but also from Paul's other letters, to have been the case. In fact, the Jewish Christian leadership, centred on Jerusalem and led by James and Peter, had been firm in a policy of admitting gentiles to the Church only if they accepted the full yoke of the Jewish Law. It was, in a way, an extreme version of Luke's own insistence on revering the Jewish past – his first phase. Luke's position now emerges as a compromise, perhaps (as was suggested) in the face of gentile Christians who saw no sense in taking Judaism on board as part of the faith centred on Jesus. So Luke tells us of Peter's own conversion on the central matter at stake (Acts 10—11) and the peaceful resolution of the dispute (Acts 15). Meanwhile, Paul's mission to gentiles is, like that which preceded it, irresistible and unstoppable. There are hazards in plenty (as Paul had recorded, chiefly in 2 Corinthians), but he and his friends survive them all – and reach Rome, where Paul's prisoner status is wholly eclipsed and he preaches the gospel 'unhindered'. It is Luke's triumphant last word. So the history ends fittingly on a note of success, just as the Gospel did. In that way there is literary as well as theological satisfactoriness.

Of course Luke knows that all is not satisfactory: Paul's only speech to a Christian audience (to the elders of the church in Ephesus, Acts 20.18–35) is full of foreboding. We should surely see this as representing Luke's fears in his own day; so that both parts of his work are designed to give succour and guidance to dispel them: both the beneficent success of Jesus in word and deed and the equal success of the apostolic mission. Those fears seem to be connected with threats to the hard-won unity of purpose and policy that Luke had described in chapter 15 (v. 29). And though it is not made explicit, it must surely be that the end in AD 70 of the Jerusalem church as (however contentiously) a visible centre for the Church had led to a sense of disarray (Luke 21.20). The completion of phase three is still awaited, the End described in Luke 17 and 21. Far more than Paul, for whom that outcome would not be long delayed, Luke finds himself preoccupied with large questions of strategy and policy for the period that remains. Again, practicalities and the shape of theology intertwine.

Finally, we may say that just as the Old Testament ethos and character of Luke 1—2 makes a bridge between phases one and two, so the apostles make a bridge between phases two and three, reproducing the acts of Jesus and, in their speeches, telling the essence of his story.

Geographical

Though it is in certain ways more explicit, Luke's temporal scheme is not in principle different from that implicit or explicit in the other early Christian writings; and its presentation is in some ways richer and more imaginative. In his geographical presentation, Luke again shows himself to be a man of his world, and a man of the Church of his world – and in this he is truly original. As we have already seen, he has a strong sense of the general situation in the Roman Empire, with its local representatives and officers (see especially the final chapters of Acts), its puppet rulers of the Herod dynasty, more of whom appear in Luke-Acts than elsewhere (e.g. the collusion of Herod and Pilate over the condemning of Jesus (Luke 23.6–12) and the similar collusion of Agrippa II and Festus over the case of Paul (Acts 25.13—26.32)), as well as its cities and sea routes. He knows the titles of office-holders and is interested in their carrying out of their duties. In all these ways, he is, with one or two provisos, at the opposite end of the spectrum of interest from the Gospel of John.

But all this local colour is set in a framework which is based on a movement from Jerusalem, the heart of Judaism and site of the temple, to Rome, capital of the known world and vital target of the Church if its mission were to succeed. Two centres, each having both its real importance and its symbolic aspect. Jerusalem was, for Luke, where the Church began. Whatever Mark meant by 'Galilee' in 16.7, i.e. whether it was literal or in some way symbolic in its reference to the future beyond the resurrection, Luke disowns it: his parallel in Luke 24.6 keeps the word but changes the sense ('Remember how he told you, while he was still in Galilee…'). For whatever reason, Matthew retained it and made a Galilean mountain the place of rendezvous for Jesus and the eleven disciples (28.16–20): Jesus had promised it and Matthew is not carrying the history any further. For Luke, and probably historically, Jerusalem was the setting of the first important centre of the Church. Only at 9.31 do we have any reference to the Christian movement in Galilee after the lifetime of Jesus; and we do not know whether this silence was based on good history or whether there were ecclesiastico-political factors that led to reticence. Or perhaps it was simply that Luke's geographical and symbolic pattern depended on fixing our minds on the Church in Jerusalem as the true heir of Judaism, worshipping God both in the temple (e.g. Acts 3.1) and in its own meetings (2.42), and meeting there in solemn council for the making of crucial decisions for the future of the mission (Acts 15).

The story ends in Rome, as we saw, with the open preaching of Paul, though, as mostly elsewhere in Acts, only his making of his case to Jews is described. Here, in the capital city of the Empire, he makes that case with candour and vehemence, and there is none of the gracious conceding that we find elsewhere to the effect that their execution of Jesus was done 'in ignorance' (3.17; 13.27; cf. Luke 23.34). The lines are firmly drawn, all the more so in this climactic and symbolic setting.

Perhaps surprisingly, there is in Luke's mind much more ambiguity over Jerusalem and the temple than there is over

Rome and the Empire. Roman officials are usually presented as friendly or mildly beneficent; while ambiguity is inherent in his attitude to Judaism as a whole. The old faith is both essential to the backing and the intelligibility of Jesus, who is no bolt from the blue, no figure open to human subjectivity, and yet it is now redirected into new and disputed channels because of Jesus' life, death and resurrection. Worse, it has failed to accept that to which its history looked forward. Jesus himself manifests both grief about Jerusalem's future fate, as he foresees its fall to the Romans in AD 70, together with the temple's destruction (Luke 19.41–44; 23.28–31), and acceptance of the inevitability and justice of that fate (21.20ff.). In rejecting him, Jerusalem has brought it upon itself. Notably, it had failed to grasp the message of the prophets, so plainly fulfilled in Jesus, as Luke has been at pains to show, in both Gospel and Acts (especially in apostolic speeches). In Acts, the disciples maintain their willing relations with the temple, but also stand up to its ruling authorities (Acts 4.1–22; 5.17–42); and in chapters 6—7, Stephen makes the most devastating case of all against the temple, so vehemently indeed that some who are otherwise persuaded that Luke-Acts is the work of a coherent mind, find his fearsome speech hard to see as consistent with the rest. But perhaps we should take it as, along with Acts 28.25–28, one side of a case. Judaism and its institutions were both God-given and damnable. It was hard for early Christians (it is perhaps hard for Christians of any age) to transcend the impulse both to welcome and to reject Judaism, whether at the level of sheer history (Christianity both grew out of Judaism and yet is very different from it, centrally in its claims about Jesus) or of theology. Christians have always, since the muddling episode of Marcion, rejected the idea that they hold a wholly new faith, the pure new gift of God, but it has remained difficult to define where to draw lines concerning what of Judaism is kept and what is discarded or transcended. It is by no means uncommon for modern Christians to appeal to provisions of the Jewish Law as authority for Christian morality, though usually with great selectivity. Matthew would welcome them more heartily than Paul or Mark; and Luke would discriminate on agreed grounds (Acts 15.20). We never transcend our past, or even know for certain how we should.

WHO THEN IS JESUS?

We have described the sweep of Luke's imagination and the scope of his mind. Clearly, he had a picture of the Christian faith that was both more 'earthed' and more strongly etched in human and geographical detail than those of either Mark or Matthew. But, as with the others, all centres on Jesus, and we turn to describe Luke's understanding of him and his role.

In formal terms, his idea of Jesus scarcely differs from those of his fellow evangelists. He makes use of the same descriptive titles like Messiah, Son of God and Son of Man, often indeed in passages taken over or shared. He adds a term that is rarer: 'saviour' (2.11; also twice in Acts). It has a background in both Jewish Scripture (regularly applied to God) and Greco-Roman usage. In early Christian writings it is found most frequently in the Pastoral Epistles where indeed there are so many similarities to Luke that, despite there being also important dissimilarities (e.g. over the role of women), he, admirer and disciple of Paul, has been put forward as their author. In 2.11 indeed there is a heaping of terms: 'Saviour... Messiah, Lord'. 'Salvation', with its underlying sense of 'rescue', is, in Luke's generous picture of things, a major way of seeing the purpose of Jesus. The Lucan story of Zacchaeus (19.1–10) shows him at his most typical. Jesus' dealings with the tax-collector give us the heart of his disposition and aims, summed up in the concluding words: 'Today salvation has come to this house.' Like so many of Luke's central ideas, it is established in his first two chapters: 1.69, 71, 77. That opening panorama of God's purpose gives us the necessary tools for understanding all that unfolds in the rest of the book (and indeed in Acts).

Apart from John, Luke is also the only evangelist to refer to Jesus as 'the Lord', sometimes adding the term in passages paralleled elsewhere (e.g. 7.19, cf. Matt. 11.2; 11.39, cf. Matt. 23.25; 22.61, cf. Mark 14.72), sometimes using it in his own work (7.13; 10.1, 41; 13.15; 17.5–6; 18.6). That Jesus was 'the Lord' may well have been the earliest Christian doctrinal decision, fixed in the mind by seeing him as fulfilling Psalm 110.1: he had been exalted by God, so he was 'my' (and so 'our') Lord: cf. the passage taken from Mark, at 20.41–44; and

Luke used the text again in Peter's first setting out of the Christian case, Acts 2.34–36.

To identify Jesus in a variety of traditional ways that express his relationships with God and the human race means having a picture, first, of his interaction with God. Luke goes further than the other evangelists in seeing this in terms of praying, importing into one Marcan context after another the statement that Jesus prays: e.g. at his baptism, 3.21; after healing a leper, 5.16; before the setting apart of the Twelve, 6.12; before asking the question about his identity, 9.18; and before the transfiguration, 9.28. No wonder then that in Luke's narrative of the passion Jesus prays not only, as in Mark and Matthew, in Gethsemane, but on the cross itself: for the forgiveness of his persecutors (23.34), and in self-surrender to the Father (23.46, in this last case quoting Scripture at his end just as he had in his opening message at 4.16ff.). As even more pervasively in John, but here explicitly, Jesus lives a life of personal devotion to God. Of course he will teach his followers how to pray, 11.2–4, and the simplicity of the prayer sums up his whole mission; but prayer is first and foremost his own act, his own way of life. Those whose hearts are 'right' similarly show devotion to Jesus: like the woman who anoints him (7.36–50) and Mary, sister of Martha (10.38–42). So in Acts, his followers will pray as he did: e.g. Stephen, 7.59–60; the church, 2.42; Paul with his close friends, 20.36. (There is more praying in Acts than, for example, in Paul's teaching in his letters!) We noted Matthew's care to 'validate' every aspect of Jesus' activity (healings, parable-telling, etc.) from Scripture. While Luke certainly takes care to emphasize the same general point (e.g. the ethos and language of the first two chapters and, explicitly, at 24. 27, 44), he prefers to demonstrate the constant validation of Jesus' life and ministry by telling us of his prayer: he and the Father are constantly in touch, living as one.

This centrality of Jesus' contact with God has its effect and counterpart in the working out of Jesus' ministry to all and sundry. While superficially its content seems much the same as in Mark and Matthew, and indeed they coincide in numerous episodes which Luke derives from Mark and shares with Matthew (and perhaps derives from him – it does not affect our present discussion), its presentation has its own distinctive features. His relationship with God is manifested in his relationship with those he meets. Putting it the opposite way round, we can tell how Luke understands Jesus' relationship with God – and how indeed he understands God – from the key characteristics of Jesus' behaviour.

It is well known, and obvious to even the casual reader, that Luke's Jesus exhibits a generosity of heart and openness to human frailty that is greater and franker than what we find elsewhere. It is of course only a matter of degree or emphasis – or, we may suppose, singleness of mind in this regard on the part of Luke. In all the Gospels, Jesus' healings and reliefs of other human ills are always at one level acts of charity; at another, they are signs of the kingdom of God, fulfilments of old expectations that in the day of consummation it would be so (e.g. Isaiah 35; 61). In Luke of course the second aspect is not absent: Jesus quotes Isaiah 61 in the crucial gathering at Nazareth in 4.16ff. But there is nevertheless a directness of dealing on the basis of need and of love which is plainer here than elsewhere. It is not that, for example, he uses the verb 'to have compassion on' more often than others (four times of Jesus in Matthew, two clear instances in Mark, twice in Luke plus once in a parable, 15.20). It is rather a matter of the simplicity of thrust in a story like the (Luke alone) stories of the raising of the widow's son (7.11–17) and of the woman who was doubled up (13.10–17). Here, as in the longer and more striking episode of the woman who anoints Jesus (7.36–50), there is the contrast between Jesus' openness and the narrow scrupulosity of others. Love triumphs over all other obligations. What is true of Jesus' conduct is also true of his parables. In that usually (but negatively – it is more the story of the Loving Father) called the Prodigal Son, there is a correspond-ing contrast between the positive attitude of the father and the grudging one of the 'good' brother (15.11–32). Similarly, the Good Samaritan story (10.25–37) hinges on the Samaritan's readiness to transcend boundaries to meet human need. As in the case of Jesus' prayer, this motif too reaches its climax in the Passion with the welcome given to the dying and penitent thief (23.43); as indeed does his healing work, in the cure of the slave's ear at the arrest (22.51).

A notable aspect of Luke's width of sympathy is the virtually equal treatment he gives to women alongside men, both in the Gospel and in Acts. Men and women are balanced in the birth stories; in 15.1–10, we have one parable about a male (shepherd), another about a female (coin-loser) (cf. 4.25–27). Again, it is a matter of accentuating a feature found throughout the Gospel tradition. In Acts, Luke's churches involve women along with men (no doubt reflecting the Pauline mission and probably the Pauline doctrine, Gal. 3.28).

A sterner side of Luke's depiction of Jesus is to be found in his emphasis on the rejection of wealth. The beginning of this aspect of Jesus' teaching is to be found in Mark (10.23–31), but in Luke it steps to the fore, in a series of episodes that are found in this Gospel alone (e.g. the parable of the rich man and Lazarus, 16.19–31; the story of Zacchaeus, 19.1–10). Luke's version of the first beatitude ('Blessed are you poor, for yours is the kingdom of God', 6.20) states the principle; and the human duty is stated, rather prosily, in Acts 20.35: 'It is more blessed to give than to receive.' Anyone who wishes to make a case for the Gospel and Acts being, despite appearances (e.g. Acts 1.1), the work of two different authors can point to the fact that, apart from that saying of Jesus reported in Acts 20, the theme of the abandoning of wealth and the snare of riches finds no place. But it may be that Luke sees it as taking a new form once Christian communities come into being. Now, one's wealth is contributed to the church's common purse and a new situation has come to birth (4.32–37), to be seen as normative for the churches. It is certainly the case that Luke can think of no wickedness fouler than failure to make one's contribution and deceiving one's fellow-Christians in this regard (5.1–11). Luke has no room for meanness of spirit, whether in Ananias and Sapphira or in, for example, the stay-at-home brother of the wandering son (15.25–32). And the ever-troubling Christian distinction between personal wealth and church wealth begins to emerge.

This at first sight surprisingly severe Lucan face has other manifestations. It is a mistake to take his openness and generosity for softness. In Luke's portrayal of him, Jesus can show a harshness of demand greater than anything found elsewhere, in expression at least: here, even wives may be forsaken for the sake

of the kingdom (18.29); and the language of 14.26 ('if anyone...
does not hate his own father and mother and wife and children
... and even his own life, he cannot be my disciple') is rigorous
in the extreme. Not surprisingly there is doubt how far it is put
in a rhetorical mode, such as is found in the prophets and
elsewhere, which is not intended to carry literal force. But surely
the key to such teaching is clear: one must choose which 'universe'
one will inhabit and loyalty cannot be divided between Jesus ('the
kingdom of God') and the 'ordinary world'.

For that world is not immediately to be brought to an end and
Christians must inhabit it, while being always aware of their
abiding loyalty. Plainly, Luke is not one for whom the End of
this present age is infinitely delayed, but nevertheless he does
think in terms of a longer prospect than was the case with, for
example, Paul (e.g. Rom. 13.11). The very writing of Acts points
to it. At Luke 9.23, he adds to the demand to take up the cross
the word 'daily': conversion is less a single act of decision (cf.
Mark 8.34) than a readiness to persevere. And this quality is itself
introduced by Luke at the end of the Sower parable (8.15,
replacing the thirty-, sixty- and hundredfold of Mark 4). Similarly,
'daily' occurs again in Luke's (but not Matthew's) form of the
Lord's Prayer (11.3). Christians are to be aware of the duties
implicit in the long haul. Luke combines a sense of 'the world
turned upside down' (Acts 17.6) – the word is concrete, it refers
to the social world, human society – with the need to be prepared
for long-term obedience. It is a demanding call, comparable to
some modern movements' demand that one live in a state of per-
manent revolution, even year after year. His ethic, easily found
attractive and heart-warming, after the model of Jesus, is no soft
touch, nor is it in the least sentimental.

All the same, Luke's Jesus is no stranger to convivial life, as
the reproach in 7. 34 (cf. Matthew 11.19) makes clear. In fact,
much of his teaching in Luke is delivered at dinner-parties, where
Jesus is a (sometimes forthright) guest: 5.29–32 (where Luke's
logic seems to slip: how could Levi, having just renounced his
property, afford such lavish hospitality?); 7.36–50; 14.1—15.32;
and notably the Last Supper itself, here an occasion of instruction
(some of it found in other Gospels in other places), 22.15–38;
finally, the Emmaus meal is, we read, the scene of some of the

most fundamental teaching of all, as far as Christian identity is concerned (24.25–27). Perhaps his model is the Socratic one of the 'symposium' where dining and teaching happily combine and reach literary expression.

Luke is at pains to show that in his lifetime, Jesus' disciples were, if sometimes failures, always encouraged and aided by Jesus, with ultimate success as their destiny (22.28–30). So Mark's dismal picture of them is much relieved (as indeed by Matthew): the eye is on the fruit of Jesus' resurrection in Acts and on the Church as a success, more and more. Even Judas' act results only from Satan's suborning (22.3); Peter's denial is a temporary lapse, soon to be reversed (22.31–32, 61), just as Jesus' calling him Satan is simply dropped (9.18–21); and failure in Gethsemane results not from callousness but from 'grief' (22.45). And the hope of mission to Israel is not closed off (recall the balance of 2.32): they too sinned in ignorance and can be forgiven (23.34; Acts 3.17). There is no softness here (see the ambiguous attitude to Jerusalem), just no shutting of doors.

At the resurrection, Luke performs one of his most daring acts of adaptation. By contrast with Mark and indeed Matthew, he tells the Emmaus story – at such length that it quite outshines the opening encounter at the tomb and gives us a kind of picture of how Christian life must be understood. It is lived in the company of Jesus and the common meal is its most typical expression: there he is to be found and there his instruction is to be received.

It appears that Luke, while no radical deviant, certainly has his distinctive vision to put before us; many of its features and indeed its whole pattern and shape take us into a different Christian world from those of Mark and Matthew. Partly, he is providing, like them, for his own church circumstances and needs; partly, he is expressing the way his own formation has led him to understand Jesus and his mission. Our business is to listen, to understand, and to sympathize. Then we shall see whether to follow. Luke certainly encourages us: as far as he is concerned, the mission cannot be stopped. Just as the women at the tomb spoke rather than remain silent (24.10), so from then on success is relentless. At Acts 14.19–20, we read of Paul suffering severe assault, so that he was left for dead; yet we hear nothing of recovery or convalescence. Next day, he simply goes on without delay where his journey takes him. It is a story of heroes who travel, we may say, with the spring-stepped tenacity of the Spirit.

5

John: The Timeless Evangelist?

No understanding of the book is possible if one loses sight of the simple fact that it is not a theological tract but a Gospel. What the divine agent 'heard' from God is disclosed not in his words but in his life; the 'what' is displayed in the 'how'. The matter of the Gospel, its true content, is indistinguishable from its form: the medium is the message.

(Ashton, 1991, p. 553)

In studies such as this, embracing all four Gospels, there is a tendency to pause on the threshold as one reaches the Gospel of John, almost as if one were moving to holier ground; and even this reference to the matter testifies to the tendency. But truly it is the desire of this book to resist any such segregation and to deny its propriety. This is not in order to demote, much less debunk, the Gospel of John, bringing it down to the level of others; rather the reverse. The aim here has been to bring out the depth of religious thought, various in shape and content, to be found in all. John is not reduced, all are enhanced.

As we saw, in the early centuries (though not from the beginning – in the second century, Gnostics liked it and many others shied off), John came to be felt to have a worth not shared by the others, partly out of regard for its sustained sublimity of thought and expression and partly because of its (apparent) chiming in with aspects of current Christian theological idiom, Platonist in broad character. The fathers who drew upon it did not see themselves as out-and-out philosophers, but as Scripture men, making great use of the Old Testament, but their inherent cast of mind made them glad that Jesus himself uttered statements that were wholly agreeable (if sometimes gnomic) to them. For we must remind ourselves that what John recorded Jesus as saying was read precisely in those terms: it was Jesus not John the evangelist who spoke. Few modern students of the Gospel, even those who believe that John's record is close to history, fail to recognize that the words ascribed to Jesus have been, to a greater or lesser degree, 'Johannized' on entering the Gospel. John was therefore to those early readers and users a gift – a mine of sacred and definitive quotations, hitting off or authorizing central convictions of faith in what was felt to be congenial language (though, as we now see, unjustly with respect to the first-century Jewish-Christian character of the evangelist whose work they read so gladly). It is no wonder, however, that Clement of Alexandria (late second century) called John the 'spiritual Gospel', contrasting it with the different level of the others. We should note that he, at least, saw it as more than a mine of statements and grasped its character as a book. We may not now agree with his judgement, but we can see what he meant and approve of his manner of appraisal.

However, you do not need to be a fourth-century father with elements of Platonist philosophy in your head to pause as you move from the other Gospels to John. The modern reader, perhaps innocent of any particular philosophical formation, is likely to see in this Gospel an odd combining of simplicity with profundity, especially in the shape of brief and pregnant statements: 'the Word was God'; 'I am the light of the world'; 'the truth shall make you free'. Statements like these seem to demand prolonged reflection which may still leave their meaning not exhausted. It is not that such statements are absent elsewhere; rather, here they seem to impress themselves more obviously upon the reader.

There is at the same time simplicity of vocabulary. (It is no wonder that teachers of the Greek of the New Testament often set pupils to turn first to this text.) The Gospel can seem almost a mosaic of a small number of key words: word, life, light, truth, love, glory. As in the First Letter of John, they tend to appear in concentrated clusters, with a particular word dominating a particular passage, almost as if being 'played with' by the author, while also reappearing elsewhere.

Readers of the Gospels are apt to divide. There are those who prefer the first three, or one or other of them, for their down-to-earthness, providing instruction on basic duties like love of neighbour, not being judgemental, paying one's taxes, and saying one's prayers – all, it seems, ideals that one may at least understand and perhaps one day attain, and of which one can approve (even if reluctantly in the case of tax-paying). Such Gospel-readers may find John too elevated, too 'advanced' in its quasi-mystical teaching and demands. Others of course, perhaps the more thoughtful and reflectively devout, will prefer the Gospel of John, taking loving one's neighbour and the duty of tax-paying for granted (almost as if it didn't take Jesus to give us instruction in such elementary matters!). For them, John is about the heart of the Christian life, leading us forward to our union with God, especially perhaps in chapters 14—17. This has been about general impressions, and the contrast is superficial; though there is some truth in the observations that have been made. It is time to get closer to facts.

The Gospel of John is indeed 'different' in certain identifiable ways, including that of vocabulary which has been referred to. In the first place, it is different in structure from the others. This writer chose to provide only a small number of episodes from Jesus' life, but to expand almost all of them by combining them, in a variety of ways, with discourse material, relating to the subject of the act at the heart of the passage. The other evangelists chose instead mostly to separate Jesus' teaching from the narrative of his deeds. This is not always so: for example, Luke's version of Jesus' visit to the synagogue at Nazareth (4.16–30), or the episode of the woman who anoints Jesus (7.36–50), or the three parables of Luke 15, which are delivered in the context of a meal. It is indeed a feature that Luke, more than Matthew or Mark, shares with John. But there is a difference, in that John's discourses spring from the character of the episode in question, as if commenting on its very nature: e.g. the bread of life teaching following the feeding of the crowd in chapter 6, or the teaching on mutual love following the foot-washing in chapter 13. And in literary style, one can draw no clear line between 'story' and 'discourse'. Moreover, John's episodes are very much fewer in number and treated much more expansively than elsewhere: John has been severely selective.

At the same time, the Gospel of John is exactly like the rest in telling the story of Jesus, from the start of his work in chapter 1, by way of a ministry of teaching and great deeds to his death and resurrection. It is, in other words, not, like the *Gospel of Thomas*, a collection of Jesus' wise and sublime teachings. It is easy so to describe (and even to 'feel') John. Yet it is not true to his reality: this is, at its heart, a narrative. Like the others, John's Gospel is an expression of the faith in the mode of 'story'. This raises the question whether this author knew the other Gospels – and then deliberately differed from them, to various degrees, in language and method – or whether, independently, he made the decision to work in this same basic mould. Academic opinion has differed, but it seems hard to deny some knowledge of one or all of the others – there are similarities with each; and at the least, John somehow knew (and wished to carry on) the tradition of writing in this mode about Jesus and faith centred on him. It may be that, in the way of a preacher, he would take a synoptic seed and have it grow into a full plant, meditatively produced: e.g. 6.51 is not unlike key words of the Last Supper in the other Gospels ('This is my body'): was this then the germ of his whole discourse on the bread of life? And might Jesus' prayer in John 17 have grown from the brief Lord's Prayer as found in Matthew or Luke? (See Lindars, 1971.)

Why he then differed so markedly must surely be connected (as in Matthew's relation to Mark) to the interests and thought-forms established in his particular Christian circle. The Church was already a diverse society by the end of the first century (indeed much earlier) and there could be no imposed uniformity. We should try to give an account of at least some aspects of the community behind this Gospel, in order to equip ourselves to form a picture of the Johannine way of putting Christian faith in narrative mode.

THE JOHANNINE COMMUNITY

We are uniquely fortunate (by the side of the other Gospels) in that we have other works by this group of Christians – the three Johannine epistles, most probably (though it is disputed) written after the Gospel, and so telling us of these Christians in a slightly later stage of their history. We can tell (from 2 and 3 John) that it is a matter of a group of distinct but closely related communities. We can also tell that they cannot maintain internal unity: 1 and 3 John are clear evidence of that. They quarrel about both doctrine concerning the nature of Jesus (1 John 2.18–22) and personalities (3 John); and they get to the point of schism – the first we know of in Christian history (though Paul got near it). There are signs that this instability is not unconnected with lack of structure and that in turn may be linked to their lofty spiritual idealism. 'Love one another' is their only moral rule: can any community live long at such a level? It is true that they have at least some officers ('the Elder' of 2 and 3 John), and leaders, we may imagine, have authority to forgive sins (John 20.23). But there is not the attention to these matters that we find on Jesus' lips and having his authority in Matthew 18.

It used to be reasonable to suppose that the Johannine cluster of churches was probably isolated, in life if not in geography, from other Christian communities. But the more we see the theological distinctiveness of the Gospels and the other early Christian writings, and the more we loosen their later forced compression into the single mould of the canon, the less Johannine 'isolation' is special. In another way too it now comes to seem feasible that they were not wholly out of contact with others. A number of writers, most notably perhaps Brown (1979), have suggested (and in some ways demonstrated) that if we read the Gospel aright, we can see the various relationships of this church, in its past and its present. So, for example, the references to John the Baptist, always so as to give him high credit yet make plain his subordination to Jesus, may indicate that this church had absorbed former followers of John and wanted people to be clear about the real relation of John to Jesus (cf. Acts 18.24—19.6; and indeed the depiction of this relation in Luke 1—2).

So also it may be that the rather arbitrary (it seems) occasional references to members of the Twelve (e.g. 14.8; 6.8) show an awareness of (and relationship with?) what Brown called 'apostolic churches', i.e. communities which had some connection to the person named. In particular, the Johannine Christians are aware of a need to show their own greater 'authenticity' (in doctrine and understanding of Jesus) than communities associated with Peter. Their own 'patron', unnamed, is the 'disciple whom Jesus loved', who, whenever it is relevant, is closer to Jesus than Peter, above all at the supper (13.23–24) and also in 'believing' at the tomb (20.8). Each of them has had his own subsequent ratification by history in different spheres, but at this early stage we have here the striking affirmation of Johannine superiority (contrast Matthew on Peter, 16.17–19): these Johannine Christians have got Jesus more 'right' than others. The point is made firmly by the beloved disciple's presence with Jesus' mother in what is surely a legacy-scene. This is then a theologically assured church; whereas, while in no way 'non-theological', Matthew may have been more concerned about 'issues' (of morality and practice) and Luke about communal relations between Jews and gentiles, and Mark was perhaps content to let his story speak for itself, but in a Pauline spirit.

There is little doubt that the intellectual roots of this church lay in one brand of Hellenistic Judaism; elevating the 'wisdom' tradition in some of its forms (see on the Prologue below) rather than the Law, but well acquainted with methods of scriptural exegesis. There is little sign that they had gone far in the direction of gentile mission (12.20–26 promises but does not emphasize), but they have, in their own distinctive way, worked out a manner of seeing Jesus which ruled out compromise with Judaism. It is a great deal more than squabbling about obedience to the Law; rather, it concerns God's whole strategy from the creation on (1.1–14). It is often suggested that the references to Jesus' followers being thrown out of the synagogue (seen as in Jesus' lifetime in 9.22 and 12.42, but in the future in 16.2) refer to a separation beginning with new clarity at the time the Gospel was written, probably after about AD 85, when at least some parts of Judaism are thought to have acted to expel Christians formally from the synagogue. This would chime in well with other informed guesses about the Gospel's date, i.e. probably not long after those of Matthew and Luke.

All this may indicate that this Gospel is, in its own quite different way, not much more removed from historical and social realities than that of Luke. At the same time, for all its 'local colour', its main interest is elsewhere, in explicit theological realities. But if one were ever inclined to read John as if it were timeless and otherworldly, it would be salutary to recall that the oldest fragment of any New Testament writing, perhaps going back as far as AD 125, is part of the Gospel of John (the Rylands fragment, papyrus 52): for John, Jesus' 'kingdom' may not be 'of this world', but the Gospel certainly is, in ways never to be ignored, however deep its doctrinal depths.

THE GOSPEL'S SHAPE

The Gospel of John is a mixed phenomenon. In part, it shows signs of orderly structure; in part, there is what looks like carelessness. For example, there is the broad division into what C. H. Dodd called the Book of Signs (2—12) and the Book of the Passion (13—21). The former consists of a series of acts by Jesus, most of them including discourse or discussion that elucidate their meaning; and the acts seem to intensify in import, from the turning of water into wine to the raising of Lazarus, itself foreshadowing the greatest 'sign' of all, the resurrection of Jesus. Yet the episodes are far from uniform. One of them, the healing of the official's son (4.46–54), is similar to episodes in the other Gospels, having no discursive material attached. Two chapters, 7 and 8, are discourse without 'sign'. In terms both of geographical moves between Jerusalem and Galilee and of the gradual intensifying of scale, with nature miracles leading on to human needs of growing severity, chapter 6 (the feeding, and the frightening storm) surely belongs before chapter 5 (the man sick for 38 years). In other words, it is as if the writing of this Gospel involved as much a 'putting together' as an 'authoring' or even careful 'editing'. So one might come to think that the episodes, here (oddly) even more clearly than in the other Gospels (for whom the theory was invented and was de rigueur), were originally independent compositions, made presumably for use in the church, and combined in due course but with imperfect skill. It is no wonder that this Gospel has provoked a number of theories, of varying complexity and ingenuity, to explain the text as it eventually came to exist. The eventual interposing of the story of the woman taken in adultery (8.1–11), which does not even come from the Johannine stable at all, is an extreme example of the fluidity in the make-up of this book.

At the same time, the thought of this church was cohesive enough to result in symbolic themes which run through episode after episode, making a counterweight to any suggestion of haphazardness in the actual making of the book itself. 'Water', for example, finds a place in chapters 2, 3, 4, 7 (vv. 38–39), 13, and 19.34. No doubt it evokes baptism, but behind the rite is an Old Testament symbolism of new fertility of life and Spirit and the coming of the new age (Ezek. 47; Zech. 14.8), and that gives us the clue to the message here: Jesus is the true source of all such good.

The Book of the Passion (to adopt Dodd's category) is itself composite, being made up of the supper discourses of chapters 13—17, involving indeed a kind of 'sign', the foot-washing in 13.1–11, and the passion and resurrection narratives in chapters 18—21. Here too all is not plain sailing. First, 14.31 ('Rise, let us go hence') makes as plain an ending as one could wish – yet the discourse continues for another three chapters. Socially, the stating of the intention to leave long anticipating the act of leaving is a phenomenon familiar to hosts. It is less credible in a literary composition. Again, untidy editing is the natural presumption, together with the prior writing of these so-called 'farewell discourses'. It must seem that the Johannine community had developed reflections on the lasting legacy of Jesus – on where his departure (if that would be quite their thought) had left them; and all these reflections, ending up homogeneous in character and message, unite in the assurance of his continuing reality among them, by way of the Paraclete, the Spirit of truth (see especially 14.12–18, especially vv. 16 and 18). In many important senses, the faith is that nothing has changed: Master and Church are one. Except, in fact, that now there is greater strength of 'works' than even in Jesus' visible lifetime (14.12).

Second, chapter 21 is generally taken to be a sort of appendix, but perhaps only in the same sense that chapters 15—17 are an 'appendix' to chapter 14. The argument is not dissimilar: as 14.31 looks like a final statement to the episode of the supper, so does 20.30–31, this time with regard to the book as a whole. Chapter 21 has, however, often been read as (unlike chapters 15—17) somehow inessential. It seems merely to tidy up a few loose ends and to add little of substance: items like the relative fates of Peter and the beloved disciple (so important, it seems, to the Johannine church) and that Marcan loose end, the nagging question (we saw how Luke bypassed it) of Jesus and Galilee and the mission there. (Did John find Luke 5.1–11 a godsend here? It would be only one of a number of fleeting similarities between these two seemingly so different works.) There is also a second ending, this time notoriously unclear, as to who is who (v. 24).

The passion story itself (18—19), while roughly comparable to the others, has its own distinctive features, most of them surely Johannine in intent. The most significant is the matter of date. Along a number of different lines of discussion, the Johannine timing, which makes Jesus' death coincide with the slaying of the lambs for passover in the temple, so that the supper is not (as in the other Gospels) the passover meal, has been held by some to be the more accurate. But it is scarcely deniable that such a coinciding would be a thoroughly typical Johannine stroke, worth writing into the story, whatever historical accuracy may have said. There are vocabulary difficulties which might prevail if John could be supposed to have a whole Septuagint to hand, but the term 'lamb of God' bestowed by John the Baptist (1.29, 35) prepares us for this most apt working out at the level of history, in John's eyes at least.

On a different level, John chooses to economize with the trial of Jesus before Jewish authorities and to concentrate on that before Pilate. This encounter enables him to explore two major themes that are close to the centre of his mind: the location of truth and the seat of real authority. For Pilate, the first is insoluble (18.38). For us, who have read the Gospel, 'truth' is located in Jesus (14.6); and we need to know that the sense is biblical – not abstract or scientific truth, but dependable reality whose repository and backer is God, now made known in Jesus. The second is an occasion less of discussion than of overt struggle between the protagonists. Jesus' authority is 'not of this world', that is, not based or grounded here. It does not in the least mean, as some would prefer it did, that religion must keep out of politics. Rather, it is a matter of the true source of the world's governance. Pilate and Jesus symbolize the choice at its most stark, in terms of Jesus' first-century world. And there is the important correlative fact: that the Jews, age-long devotees, guardians and prophets of God's rule, choose Pilate's side (19.15), making the ultimate act of apostasy. The Jewish Christians of the Johannine church are as bitter about Jesus-rejecting Jews as those of the Matthean. In that sense and to that degree, the bitter debate is still intra-Jewish, though, as we saw, it is on the edge of ceasing to be so (9.22), with the churches more and more gentile in composition and Christians no longer welcome in the synagogue. It may seem, from our perspective, remarkable that coexistence had lasted in some places so long – a tribute in a way to the breadth of Judaism's inclusiveness at this time. Yet the Johannine church knew of movements across the boundaries and traces their possibility in the context of the life of Jesus: see the figure of Nicodemus in 3.1–21, 7.50 and 19.39; and the discussions in chapters 7—8. Surely they correspond to that church's experience.

This aspect of the debate between Jesus and Pilate in fact leads us to another pervasive theme in John (which again makes us think that, however varied in their origin may be some of the episodes included in the Gospel, they testify to a high level of concentration in this church on a specific range of ideas and themes): that of 'the world'. The word *kosmos* in John nicely illustrates what can be seen as an unresolved tension in the Johannine mind – it was virtually inevitable in a community which combined largeness of vision, to the point of universality, with smallness and 'fraughtness' of immediate scene and prospects. So 'world', referring much more to human society than to physical setting, carries a variety of tones. Sometimes it is expansive, positive and good, the object of God's universal creativity and love (1.10; 3.16) and of his salvific intention (12.47); sometimes it is where Jesus does not belong (18.36) or that which is hostile to Jesus and his people, the scene of 'the evil one' (14.17, 19; 17.14, 15); sometimes it seems to be viewed neutrally, simply the stage on which all is played out (17.5). The element of hostility or rejection of the world, easily explained, without looking further, by the Johannine church's embattled situation, as a minority of Christians within another minority of Jews, gives rise to the suggestion that this community was en route to a gnostic view of the universe, viewing it as scarcely the handiwork of a beneficent creator (see Käsemann, 1971). John 17, on which the case for such an interpretation concentrates, does indeed seem to encourage a perspective of this kind. But, allowing for the surrounding pressures, we can see that the Judaism-based theology, with its positive view of God's supreme creative and saving role towards the world, is more fundamental and prevails: the book begins by affirming it and centring it on Christ.

The Prologue, 1.1–18, may well have come into being late, to introduce and appropriately to epitomize the whole. It has its own Johannine-type key term: 'word' (*logos*), not used in this sense beyond this passage. Its provenance lies in the wisdom tradition of Judaism, which had wide ramifications in Jewish literature: Psalm 33.6; Isaiah 55.10–11; Wisdom of Solomon 9.1; 18.15 – a passage that most of all makes us ready for a personalizing of the *logos*, which takes flesh-and-blood form in the Jesus of this Gospel. The Prologue seems to be constituted loosely as a reflection of Genesis 1, starting with the identical expression, 'In the beginning', and leading through the creation of 'light' and 'life' to Jesus, as if a new Adam (v. 14; cf. 19.5). The oddly intrusive (as it seems to us) references to the Baptist surely reflect how close to the front of the Johannine mind this aspect of the community's past or present was and remained.

THE THEOLOGICAL OUTLOOK OF JOHN

So far this chapter has been concerned with setting the scene for what follows. But as in the theatre the scene-setting can prepare us for the play that is about to be staged, so here these introductory matters should help us to understand the distinctive message of the book. Indeed, a number of its important aspects have already come before us.

This account will be topical or diagrammatic rather than following the Gospel's text in order, though it happens that the opening passage of the Gospel will come before us first. But before we embark, we should stand back and consider the nature of the enterprise, on which we now engage for the fourth time. First, we need to be clear what we mean our subject to be. It is capable of a number of definitions. It might, for example, be about how being human looks in the light of John. Whether we come to this Gospel in a religious spirit or not, there is no denying that this is a subject on which it throws light. But it is unlikely that the evangelist himself would have given it as his chief interest in writing. More obviously, it is about the evangelist's understanding of God in the light of Jesus, and anything else that is included or achieved is a by-product, however interesting or significant.

But the procedure remains complex or indirect. After watching three other evangelists attempting the same task, we know that there is a great deal of room for subjectivity and diversity; and we are not to be embarrassed or grudging about that, for there is no alternative: to exist and to think is to intrude or to present one-self! In attempting to 'understand God in the light of Jesus', a writer (or reader, thinker, or person praying) works at two removes: as we read the Gospel, it is a matter of us looking at the evangelist looking at Jesus (and God through him). And of course, as was suggested, we cannot avoid looking back at ourselves in the light of the task as a whole. How does what we have seen reflect our own self-understanding?

As we saw at the beginning of this chapter, there is a strong impulse to view this evangelist's tackling of the work as more 'profound' than that of his fellows. Is there sense in that, or is it just a legacy of the way this Gospel has been used (and theologically privileged) in the Church down the centuries? We have seen that it is certainly false to take this Gospel as uniquely theological, either in intention or in achievement: all four were articulating faith thoughtfully by way of the story of Jesus. But we might sense a greater breadth of vision here – the word 'cosmic' springs to mind. Still we need to be careful. Luke too had his own kind of universality, in both time and space (so far as these were open to him at the time). And no doubt some modern readers may relate to his concrete, pictorial sense of time and space more readily than to what may seem the more abstract manner of John. We are after all creatures of time and space and should never lose sight of that when we turn to faith. Christian theology does not necessarily benefit from abstraction, or rise thereby to a 'higher plane'. All the same, John seems to offer profundity by way of an unparalleled concentration of images or metaphors for what Jesus signifies for us and for the 'world' on behalf of God.

So let us offer the thesis that it is the concentration which is at the heart of John's special success and impressiveness. In say-ing this, we should not for a moment abandon the historical realism about John which we have brought to mind: the book came from a particular community at a particular time. Nor is it a matter of his being philosophically more acute in a way that a modern European with an education in the humanities can feel comfortable with ('John was one of us, and that is to his credit'). To say that is to uproot him from his time and to engage in the kind of domesticating that began in the patristic age, for both good and ill: it was helpful at the time – and yet misleading.

(Anyway, today we are not all philosophers of any kind at all, and the old echoes do not resonate.) So we return to the formulation adopted earlier, and should read it neither more nor less ambitiously than its words go: among the evangelists John gives us an unparalleled concentration of images or metaphors for what Jesus signifies.

To put the point in another way: John sees Jesus as the plenary mediator, occupying all conceivable (that is, to John) 'mediatorial space' between God and us (= the world) – and doing it effectively, that is to say, for 'salvation', or, in one of John's formulations, to 'take away the sins of the world' (1.29), or in another, to bring us to the Father so that mutual love may be established (17.26). In that way, he is not elaborating an abstract scheme, as if for its own sake in terms of intellectual satisfaction or elegance. John believes that what he writes of has been effective and remains so: we benefit in relation to God. In that way, his concern (i.e. with God's saving 'work') is fundamentally Jewish in its emphasis, even though its way of achievement is new and of course, as he knows, deeply controversial. Because of that, it is necessary that he should present as watertight a case (as total a filling of mediatorial space) as he possibly can. He must leave no leaky places where the insufficiency of Christ may appear.

We may expound this integrated and comprehensive case in terms of a series of 'levels' or 'circles' in mediatorial space. This is what was meant by saying we should proceed in a diagrammatic way rather than simply going through the text in order. We shall begin with the widest 'circle' of all and move gradually inwards.

The 'world' or creation as a whole

Recall that John's interest is in humanity rather than in 'nature' – only Paul among the New Testament writers (and only momentarily) has much feel for that (Rom. 8.19–23; but cf. Rev. 21.1). Jesus is the agent of its making and its saving; the former is put by way of his taking on the traditional mediatorial mantle of 'wisdom' or 'word', both expressing the rational intentionality of God in the making of the universe (Prov. 8. 22–31; Wis. 9.1–2): it was not haphazard or arbitrary. John did not invent the placing of this mantle on the shoulders of Jesus of Nazareth. It had been done decades before by Paul, at least in 1 Corinthians 1.24 and 8.6; and the Pauline tradition maintained it in Colossians 1.15–20. In John it seems more explicit, in the opening 18 verses; and it emerges again in 5.46 and 8.58: Jesus the Word, now 'made flesh' (1.14), was the agent of God in creation and then in the life of Israel. We may explain this improbable idea (as it may seem) in terms of Jewish tradition whereby all vital mediators of God could be seen as pre-existent and eternal (e.g. the Law, ultimately delivered to Moses; the design of the temple, similarly; and the Messiah's 'name'). Was this not a way of expressing the 'ultimacy' of these things as expressions of the divine character and purpose? If that is right, then to say less of Jesus would be to limit or relativize his importance in a way that, if one shared this manner of thinking, would be intolerable. Of course, then, he was God's 'word' from the beginning – and was 'made flesh and dwelt among us' (1.14).

The realism of this manner of faith, as taken into the tradition of Christian doctrine, is depicted, for example, among the carvings in the north porch of Chartres Cathedral, where a Jesus-like figure looks down lovingly upon a half-recumbent young man whom he appears to be waking. It is not immediately apparent to the uninformed (or to the modern believer who has perhaps lost the realism of this style of faith) that this is a depiction of the Word creating Adam (Gen. 1.26). We may reflect how easily the evangelist might (with perhaps a little education in medieval styles of expression) have grasped what was here presented to him. Fourth-century Christians embraced the concept readily: but how many of their modern successors, reciting the Nicene Creed, see 'by whom all things were made' as referring to Christ, the creative 'word'? Unless such an idiom happens to have become natural to us, we may wish to say that such a manner of thought is poetic, or even fanciful – 'just an image'. For John, it was vital: without it, Jesus as God's truly comprehensive agent would have been amputated from the start, and with respect to the deepest and widest dimension of things. We should note, however, that the need for such a consideration seems not to have occurred to the other evangelists; but then the 'shape' of their thought was different – neither better nor worse, but different.

Israel – Law

Here is the second 'circle', lying within the first, which was the 'world'. However comprehensively the role and significance of Israel have been transcended by Christ, for John the former is still a fundamental presence and, in its way, pervasive. Jesus is 'the saviour of the world' (4.42) but nevertheless 'salvation is from the Jews' (4.22). Israel is crystallized in its Scriptures. So John, like his fellow evangelists, quotes and alludes to Scripture (notably the psalms – perhaps they were among his meagre stock of scrolls), seeing Jesus as fulfilling its words and images. Some of his uses are as ingenious and skilled as Matthew's; for example, his working with the Jacob (= Israel) story from Genesis 28.10–17, with ladder and angels and a place which is 'the gate of heaven'; cf. John 1.51. It was a text which handed John his own doctrine on a plate. His references to Scripture are also bold: 'If you believed Moses, you would believe me, for he wrote of me.' Put that alongside 8.58, 'Before Abraham was, I am', and we see that, for John, Jesus not only fulfils Scripture but was also present within it, just as he was the agent of the world's creation (1.1–3). Paul knows the same doctrine (e.g. 1 Cor. 10.4), but among the evangelists only John clearly holds it. It is a way of seeing Jesus as 'fulfilling' Scripture which is more intense, more internal, than that which we find in, for example, Matthew.

Israel's life, especially as God's own people, centred on the Law, his supreme gift. It was necessary therefore for John to show us Jesus as taking over its place: 'the law was given through Moses; grace and truth came through Jesus Christ' (1.17). So also many of the major images which Jesus takes to himself were attached in Scripture to the Law: 'light of the world' (8.12; cf. Ps. 119.105); 'way, truth, life' (14.6; cf. Ps. 119.37, 43, 142). The first of John's 'signs' (the changing of water into wine, 2.1–11) no doubt signifies precisely Jesus' superseding of the old dispensation of the Law, so that John establishes the point early in his narrative. He reaffirms it at the end, again including the mother of Jesus to represent that which is now handed over to the community of Jesus (19.25–27). The old is not abolished or forgotten, but certainly transcended.

So it is that Jesus fulfils not only the Scriptures but also the hopes of Israel. It is made clear in the sequence of titles for Jesus (Messiah, king of Israel, etc.) rehearsed in 1.35–51 amid the preliminaries for his witness on the stage of the world at large (chapters 2—12), before the withdrawal to the enclosed setting of the Church in chapters 13—17, where the terms of the future are laid down for ever. It is made clear too in the mid-point confession entrusted to Martha at 11.27 (Messiah, son of God) and in the final summary, 20.30–31; and it is demonstrated from time to time, notably in the entry to Jerusalem (12.12–19), and sometimes with irony, as in the muddled Jewish discussion about the Messiah's provenance in 7.40–44.

Temple

Observance of the Law centred until AD 70, and still in Jewish hope and theory, on the temple, at least as far as its vital sacrifical and commemorative aspects were concerned. So Jesus fulfils the temple's place. This point too is established early: John transfers the so-called cleansing of the temple from its eve-of-passion place in the other Gospels to what is for him a more prominent and point-making position. He is keen to get all major aspects of his case established near the start of his narrative. (We may compare this move to Luke's transfer of Jesus' visit to the synagogue in Nazareth from its later position in Mark (6.1–6; still later in Matthew) to a key place at the start of the ministry, 4.16–30. We can also note John's indifference to the perspectives of modern historical reconstruction, with its focusing on the temple incident as the possible trigger for Jesus' arrest.)

Similarly, in John, Jesus 'occupies' the temple to be the scene of his teaching which he delivers against formidable odds (again, there is a hint of this in Luke 2.41–52; 19.47—20.47). As his Father's house (2.16), it is his true place and he is its true lord (7.14—8.59); and of course it is the heart of the city of his rejection. More ingeniously, to our minds at least, Jesus fulfils the hopes for the role of the temple when God's day of restoration comes. His life-giving mission is seen in terms of the image of abundant water, flowing from beneath the temple (Zech. 14.8; Ezek. 47). Jesus speaks of it in 7.37–39, linking it with the other image for new force and vitality (the Spirit), and he enacts the sense of it on the cross (19.34–35). And the water's life-giving role will be fulfilled in the baptism of his followers (3.1–15; cf. 1 John 5.6–8).

There is another manifestation of this motif. In John 4.1–26, there are what appear at first sight to be two disparate themes, the 'living' (life-giving) water which Jesus will give and the location of true worship. In the light of the other passages that have been referred to, we can see that the two merge into one. Life-giving water, signifying the Spirit, will flow from the temple, and flows too from Jesus, both historically and sacramentally (and the former dimension is by no means negligible for this writer); and the temple is the location of worship which, truly offered, is to centre on Jesus: 'God is spirit, and those who worship him must worship in spirit and in truth' (4.24; cf. 14.6).

There is one further circle, narrower still.

The feasts observed at the temple

John goes to considerable lengths to show how Jesus 'fulfils' or takes over the great festivals of Judaism, chiefly passover and tabernacles. These are pilgrim feasts, observed at the temple by large numbers of Jews from Palestine itself and from the dispersion. John pays most attention to the former, telling of Jesus attending three passovers (2.13; 6.4; 13—19). Incidentally, it is only this feature of John, not paralleled elsewhere, which leads to the common belief that Jesus' ministry was three years long; and the interesting question is whether John's interest (or knowledge) was historical at all or whether he was simply concerned to emphasize Jesus' role as heir to the feast's significance – in our terms, letting him fill yet another corner or circle of 'mediatorial space'. In other words, while it is very probable that Jesus did indeed go to Jerusalem to the feasts on numerous occasions during his life, that is not John's concern; any more than it is, for example, Mark's concern to deny it when, for his own different theological intention, he tells of only the single visit which is his journey ('way') to death, or Luke's when he tells of a visit at the age of 12 which is a kind of tableau of Luke's sense of Jesus' relation to Judaism, dependent yet transcending.

It is of course the final passover that dominates the Gospel and indeed this aspect of John's presentation. Jesus, in his sacrifical death, is the culmination and goal of all passovers, the commemoration of the liberation of God's people from Egyptian slavery (cf. Jesus' final words, 'It is finished', i.e. completed, achieved, 19.30). As we saw, its timing differs from that in the other Gospels with the effect that Jesus' death coincides with the mass slaughter of animals for the family meal that follows, and John's irony comes through in the busy oblivion of the passover pilgrims to the enactment of what John sees as their true liberation. Details of the death recall the law of passover: 19.36, cf. Exod. 12.46.

Other festivals feature too, unnamed in 5.1 and that of the dedication in 10.22. But tabernacles is the only other one that is given clear prominence (chapters 7—8). We note the theme of light (8.12), perhaps alluding to the use of torches at the feast, and the occurrence of the verb 'abide' (8.31–35), which admittedly is used more densely elsewhere, especially in chapter 15, perhaps pointing to the contrast between the ephemeral nature of the temporary booths erected for the feast and the permanence that Jesus brings.

JESUS AS DIVINE

One other matter demands comment in this survey of John's presentation of faith in terms of the story of Jesus. It is his bestowal on Jesus of divine status. It is by far the clearest such statement in the early Christian writings that were taken into the New Testament. The relevant texts (1.1, 18; 20.28; together with 10.30 and indeed the pervasive sense of Jesus' 'oneness' with the Father, especially in chapter 17) were a gift to later Christian theological formulation. But the question is: did John have in mind quite what later doctrine took him to mean and used him to warrant? If we bring historical sense to the question, it seems remarkable that a Christian of Jewish formation could arrive at such a conclusion or even make any sense of it. 'The Lord our God, the Lord is one' (Deut. 6.4) is bedrock.

But as L. W. Hurtado has shown (1998), by our period (and in various respects for a long time) the monotheism of Judaism, though essentially intact, was modified by speculative belief in various 'escorts' of God, acting as mediators or manifestations of the divine in various respects and for various purposes. Such escorts or agents ranged from angels to personified qualities like 'wisdom' or 'word' and exalted heroes like Moses or Elijah. Conceptually 'one and all alone', God was nevertheless not, we might say, in the least lonely! Several passages of Scripture manifest fluidity between these categories: are the three 'men' of Genesis 18 human, angelic or 'as good as' God himself? In Judges 13, there is fluidity about the identity of the visitor: is he an angel (v. 3), a man of God (v. 6), or God himself (v. 22)? And was 'wisdom' a quality inherent in God, like the wisdom of a human being, or was it a distinguishable entity (e.g. Prov. 8.22–31)?

In such a climate, well-developed in aspects of first-century Judaism, how does the giving of the term 'God' to Jesus stand? We should note that in all three cases where it appears in John, there is both an affirming and a denying or qualifying. In 1.1, the 'word' is both distinguished from God ('with God') and identified with him ('the Word was God'). In 1.18, there is a scarcely-to-be-decided textual issue, some manuscripts having 'only-begotten Son', others 'only-begotten God'. Taking the latter option, we may say that the introduction of the adjective has the effect of both affirming and yet modifying the appellation 'God'. In 20.28, the climactic instance, we note that a little earlier, at 20.17, a firm distinction is drawn between Jesus and God; the effect being to modify the apparently strong statement in the later verse.

It has been convincingly suggested that the background to this mode of discourse lies in the Jewish law of agency, whereby, in a pre-telephonic and pre-email society, a business or other representative must, for practical purposes, be given authority to speak for his principal, so that 'a man's agent is as the man himself'. What is more, it is apparent that, normally, a man's son, the expectant heir, is the best agent of all: they are at one (cf. John 10.30) in intentions and interests. This vivid, prosaic and convincing image seems to be what is involved in John's usage, and 13.16, with its mini-parable drawn from life, seems to confirm it: 'a servant is not greater than his master; nor is he who is sent greater than he who sent him'; this, rather than what would be an anachronistic metaphysical scheme (see Borgen, 1986).

In this context, we should consider the appearance in John (alone) of the expression, used with solemnity and deliberateness, 'I am'. Does it not reflect the divine name revealed to Moses at the burning bush (Exod. 3.14)? There is the initial difficulty with this attractive and apparently obvious suggestion that in the Septuagint version the translation means literally 'I am the existent one' – it has gained a marginally philosophical tone, and 'the existent one' is given as the name itself; but then, John may not have used what came to be standardized as the Septuagint text. In any case, there is doubt that this really lies behind John's usage.

The passages concerned fall into two categories: those with a predicate, mostly one of the great Johannine terms or images – 'I am the bread of life; the light of the world; the resurrection and the life; the way, the truth and the life' (6.35; 8.12; 9.1; 11.25; 14.6); and those that are absolute, like 8.28 and 58. As we saw, the images are drawn from long Jewish usage and are standard currency for describing the Law – and also for characterizing the figure of 'wisdom', who feeds God's faithful (Prov. 9.5) and gives them a 'way' to walk in (Prov. 9.6). So of course Jesus steps into the accepted roles of God's wisdom, which is the alternative term for his word.

As for the absolute uses of 'I am', we should surely look for precedent to Isaiah 40—55, where there is frequent solemn use of the identical (and standard) Greek (*ego eimi*), to signify God's self-affirmation, sometimes indeed repeated to strengthen the effect ('I am I am'): e.g. Isaiah 43.10, 13, 25; 45.19; 46.4; 51.12 (some cases apparent only in the Septuagint). As God's plenipotentiary agent, Jesus speaks as the one who 'sent' him.

It follows moreover, in Johannine perception, that this position is reproduced and perpetuated in and for those whom Jesus himself 'sends' in his stead: 20.21. So too they are 'one' as Jesus and the Father are 'one' (in purpose and deed): 10.30; 17.11 etc. Indeed, all the major images that in the first part of the book (chs 2—12) characterize the relationship of Father to Son and are proclaimed on the world's stage are reproduced in the Supper Narratives (chs 13—17) and extended to embrace Jesus' 'own';

with the Spirit (Paraclete) as the joining factor. So, for example, Jesus does the Father's 'works' (5.19–20), and the Christians will do even greater 'works' (14.12); the Father loves Jesus (10.17), his followers must love one another (13.34).

The more far-reaching this perspective (and it seems almost total, carried through with rigour), the more we see the power of John's 'realized eschatology'. That is, the transformation of all things that was envisaged, with such great confidence, in Jewish eschatology and especially in the current apocalyptic literature, is seen by John as planted within the world by and in Jesus, and then by and in his followers. This is so to the extent that, with the exception of a very few brief passages about a hope for a God-given future, put in terms of resurrection (e.g. 5.24–27), John barely casts his eyes beyond the limits of the narrative he writes and the world of Jesus and his own which it chiefly depicts – it being understood that for John the Christian community which he knows surely lives still within its terms. No wonder then that the sole moral precept that he needs to issue is 'that you love one another' (13.34); for others, 'neighbours', after the wider vision of the Good Samaritan story (Luke 10.25–37), are outside the company of faith. We need to understand that the latter is for John the focus less of moral than of theological or existential interest (and in this way he is in fact closer to the original sense of the command to love the neighbour in Leviticus 19.18, where the neighbour meant the fellow-Israelite).

In this intensity of the presence now of the things of 'the End', John goes beyond the other evangelists. He even goes beyond Paul who shared, and indeed initiated, this sense of the present establishment of the age to come (e.g. new creation, 2 Cor. 5.17; gift of the Spirit, Rom. 8.4, 14). The question is then raised: how important for the logic of John's teaching (as distinct from his inherited assumptions) was Jesus' resurrection, that act which took the Christian vision beyond the time of Jesus himself? The greater the weight that John puts on Jesus' embracing of his own within the web of his own forming of them (chs 13—17) and on Jesus' death as the act of 'glory', when God's character is fully displayed (John 13.31; 17.1–5), the less of a role there is for anything beyond. In Jesus, God has given and done all. This goes beyond the other Gospels in its creative following of the logic of a Christian understanding of Jesus, though perhaps in their very act of the writing of the story, they too have gone further than they understood to bring the End forward, to be among us in Christ: eschatology cannot be as it had been; and, as we see, John's 'doctrine' goes beyond that which he himself can quite live with as he writes his narrative: chapters 20—21 are part of his text. (We note again that he was anticipated by Paul, for whom baptism unites the believer in Jesus' resurrection, here and now, Rom. 6.3–11.)

In this move of his, there is, for us, a taste of modernity; and it is certainly true that it has little in common with much of the popular Christian tradition, with its emphasis on death and its aftermath until the Last Judgement. John gives little justification for the dooms on the west walls or in the west windows of the churches of Europe; for the judgement is already past for Jesus' own, done in the act of faith (3.17–19).

There may then be a final question whether, despite his literary form, John's Gospel is truly a 'narrative' in the same sense as the other Gospels. Is this truly a presenting of faith in 'story' rather than 'doctrine' mode? In form, it certainly is; but does it 'matter' to this writer that it should be so? Yes, in the vital sense that his concern is with the Word who 'was made flesh and dwelt among us', and 'the world', where life is in the narrative mode, is the scene of his human existence and his death and, behind that, the object of his love (3.16).

6

Believing via the Story: Costs and Rewards

The words of a dead man
Are modified in the guts of the living.
(W. H. Auden, 'In Memory of W. B. Yeats',
1976, p. 197)

Thoughts and events, beliefs and facts, we tend to assume,
antedate narrative and text. We are fascinated by and seek
to establish our identity on a non-narrative, non-textual
reality, and we consider narrative texts to be prisons where
facts and ideas are kept and from which they must be freed.
(Kort, 1988, p. 142)

From one point of view, this book has been a study in subjectivity,
with the Gospels as the chief illustrations. Their only interest in
this regard is the relative novelty and, in some circles, unpopu-
larity of this way of looking at them. As we have seen, since the
second century, it has been usual, with minor qualifications, to
see them as broadly of a single mind. This judgement continues
to have its powerful advocates, even in the world of the modern
study of the Gospels and of early Christianity. For example,
Hengel (2000) followed ancient tradition in continuing to see
the four Gospels as truly complementary; and Caird (1994) set
out as the most appropriate picture of the New Testament
writings (including the Gospels), the idea of a colloquy, an
apostolic conference. It is as if they were people discussing a series
of great themes and each contributing to the talk from his own
angle. Apart from the fact that Caird himself, as author-chairman
of the imagined colloquy, having a book to organize, set the
agenda, there is the question whether this can be the most
appropriate model for the early Church. At any such conference,
it must seem, there would have been a good deal of storming out.
The chairman is then enforcing their continued attendance and

compelling a kind of posthumous agreement. It has been our contention that, leaving aside, for example, the crucial turmoil of Paul in relation to Peter, James and their supporters, the Gospels themselves are the result of profound disagreements. Matthew and Luke wrote their books because they were not content with the Gospel of Mark. And, supposing he knew at least some of his predecessors, John certainly chose to go his own very different way.

Secular historians recognize in such proceedings as Caird proposed an instance of the well-known phenomenon, the so-called Whig interpretation of history: that is to say, the past viewed simply as leading up to the present desirable state of affairs – in politics, perhaps parliamentary democracy or human rights or the rule of law for everybody. All crinkles in the actual processes of the past are ironed out as one contemplates the supposedly unstoppable drive to the desirable destination that has been reached.

It is a view of the past of which religious historians, notably when they double up in the role of church leaders, have often been past masters – in any number of different and incompatible interests. In all such cases, the stakes are high, and in every instance, divine backing may be claimed. (For the classic discussion of the phenomenon, see Wilken, 1971.)

We have seen how inadequate historically is any such account of the formation of the Gospels. Closely related as at least three of them are, they did not arise out of any intention to collaborate in a common venture, but rather out of attempts (in the cases of Matthew and Luke) to improve on and, in certain important ways, undermine the teaching of at least one predecessor, Mark. It was the start of the Whiggish process when they were joined in a collection of Gospels, taken to be harmonious contributions to a single cause. In a way, of course, they were exactly that: all were witnessing to their authors' faith in Jesus as God's determinative agent for salvation. But when it came to further thought on the matter, they took different and sometimes contradictory lines, on subjects of crucial importance. Moreover, it seems clear that by the time they came to be treated as a unit – the Four Gospels – their theological distinctiveness, indeed their theological character, in the sense of being products of distinctive theological minds, was no longer recognized, their varied voices no longer heard. Indeed, when it came to serious theological statement, they were, as we saw, scarcely used at all. In so far as they were drawn upon for theological purposes (it was chiefly the Gospel of John), it was by way of isolated statements, read as if written in the time and culture of the quoters, and as if Jesus' words were recorded verbatim.

It has always seemed to most readers that 'inspiration' by the Spirit can only mean such direct travel from voice to book, with Jesus' audience and the author as no more than conduits ensuring safe arrival. It is a peculiarly untrusting and unecclesiastical view of such a God-given process. Moreover, in our perspective here, it means that a document comes to be used for a purpose its author never intended. That, of course, is often perfectly legitimate: authors have no exclusive rights to their products. It is, however, unhappy when the adopted purpose is directly contrary to what the writing set out to achieve. No good using Shakespeare's *Twelfth Night* as evidence for the state of affairs in Illyria or *Macbeth* for light on Scottish history in the eleventh century. No good reading a Gospel to get the kind of timeless utterance of Jesus which it never meant to give and which, out of its original context, would be in any case difficult for us to receive.

Even as late as the work of John Donne (1572–1631), when the beginnings of a candid historical approach to Scripture were not far distant, there is little sign of movement in such a direction. Scripture was essentially (despite obvious problems for which there was a tradition of elucidation) a unified whole, whose authors were the 'secretaries of the Holy Ghost' (see Edwards, 2001, pp. 307–10); and 'use' meant devout quarrying in the text for the illumination of a faith that was in fact otherwise conceived and expressed (chiefly in church documents of various kinds).

Subjectivity among the evangelists, in the sense that each wrote his own book, expressing his own sense of faith in Jesus for his own church and personal circumstances, has been our subject. In terms even of the history of the Church, it is in some ways a microscopic subject: these brief books, however important in esteem, however extolled (rather than comprehendingly used) as theological authorities, however constantly read in liturgy, are small in relation to the weight of developed theological writing by individuals and by churches; and, as

Chapter 1 brought out, Christian doctrinal elucidation and formulation have worked largely on principles that ignored the greater part of the Gospels. Only recently has there been the chance to read them as theological productions in their own right – put of course in the still uncon-genial 'story' mode.

Subjectivity is likely to have affected readers of this book, as intellectual or spiritual sympathy arose with one Gospel rather than the rest. Like the Christians in Corinth, it will have been a case of 'I belong to Mark, I belong to Matthew, I belong to Luke, or I belong to John' (cf. 1 Cor. 1.12). While no modern reader shares the setting of thought and culture of any of them, one can nevertheless feel greater or lesser affinities to this or that style of being a Christian. It is not fanciful to see each of them as, in effect, a long-unrecognized fount of one way of being Christian, i.e. of viewing and responding to God, Jesus and human life, that has persisted through Christian history. In different Christian settings of time and place and church, the degree of affinity felt in relation to one or other of the evangelists will doubtless vary, but each of them surely has those who welcome his world of thought and his style of faith.

While the differences of theology between the Gospels can be overdone, claims for their 'essential unity' have an affinity with the view from the distant satellite showing that Europe and Asia are really much the same place. In the case of Caird, it was achieved by the tactic of the cheerful and forceful chairman who insists on a successful outcome of the meeting at any cost. And in the case of the Gospels, we might read each in turn, entering with sympathy into its particular theological and religious 'world', with the aim of humbly allowing each to correct the impact of the other. Who are we, after all, to challenge the fourfold Gospel provision, even if it was arrived at without our understanding of the diversity (and hostility) of voices it contains?

The weakness with this eirenic proposal is that it may be necessary for us to make choices. Some of the issues on which the evangelists differ (and because of which one was led to write in order to correct and supplant another) are still with us; not of course in their first-century form, but in essence. Indeed, these are the factors which led us to feel an affinity with one or another in the first place. Let us consider some of the choices which we can scarcely avoid, putting them in the form of questions.

1   Is it equally adequate to Christian faith to see life as under detailed regulation and strict judgement (Matthew) as to see us all as under both sin and abundant grace (Mark)?
2   Is it equally adequate to see Jesus as wonderfully generous to the undeserving or inadequate (Luke) and as the saviour who brings God to us and us to God (Mark, John)? In this case both may 'please' us, but what about adequacy or profundity of theological approach?
3   Is it equally adequate to see Jesus as mysteriously 'other' (Mark, John) and as the good companion (Luke)?
4   Or to see his death as 'glory' (John) and his death as (however much 'meant') still humanly tragic (Luke), or as simply scripturally inevitable and yet a wicked act (Matthew)?

Alternatives such as these mean that there are choices to be made, lessons to be learnt, and not just instinctive affinities to be followed. At the same time, of course, it would be draconian to say that only one Christian path is valid, only one kind of Christian lifestyle and mind-style to be encouraged. Even the most authoritarian churches and traditions usually include (even where they do not encourage) different emphases and styles, though smaller sects have often begun on a narrow path (encouraged indeed by the Jesus of Matt. 7.14 who might well have shared their spirit).

Such choices might encourage the conclusion that, for the sake of order, the 'credal' or 'doctrine' mode of Christian statement and Christian faith is the more satisfactory one. That is, Christian teaching and statement are best found as a unified, agreed and authorized whole; whether in short formulas like creeds or catechisms or in fully argued works of systematic theology by accredited experts.

However, the position is still more complicated. Not only are there choices to be made in the present, perhaps prompted by an imaginative reading of the Gospels. There are also choices to be made as one surveys the Christian past, when, for the most part the 'doctrine' mode went largely unchallenged, at least in the official working of the Church. Take, for example, the subject of attitudes to death. It is undeniable that, for a variety of social as well as religious reasons, over long periods of Christian history a preponderant weight of intellectual, devotional (and financial) attention has been given to the subject of life after death. One has only to think of the huge investment in prayers for the dead in Europe, as described for late medieval England in, for example, Duffy (1992) or for eighteenth-century France in McManners (1981). How different are the spiritual and theological attitudes revealed there from the proportions of belief, and even the senses of words, from those found in, for example, Paul, for whom one's significant 'death' came in one's baptism (Rom. 6.3–11), so that physical death was reduced to a future incident that paled by comparison with that which had already taken place, or in the Gospel of John, for whom the move to faith was one 'from death to life' (5.24). Not only words but also perspectives were thus transformed, and it does not exaggerate to say that in many crucial respects the later developments represent a different religion or at any rate so different a version of the old that, whatever the continuities of official faith, the 'stories' actually told and believed were quite different. It is probably naive to say that if there had been a more lively attention to the 'story' mode at earlier stages, such loss of the valuable, even essential early perceptions might not have taken place. It is interesting that the later decline of the styles of belief on this subject that are revealed in Duffy and McManners came as a matter of theology ('doctrine' mode) in Luther and Calvin and those who followed them, and a matter of sensibility ('story' mode?) in other parts of the Church, where one does not hear now of chantries or very much about perpetual masses for departed loved ones.

The Gospels, by their character, the way they 'work', and the way they came into being, suggest that looser mode of Christian statement, that of 'narrative' or 'story', which, paradoxically, might have had a better chance of holding on to the essence of such vital perceptions than alternative ways of proceeding. One may draw an intelligible distinction between that which may 'instruct' one and that which may 'form' one. The former suggests a process of acquisition whose completion represents an achievement. One now knows and grasps what one did not know and grasp before, but one may well not have become (as we put it) a different person. The latter suggests a process of more interior growth and formation, the gradual and never-ending business of consideration and contemplation of that which can never be exhausted. It seems that the former may be less formative of the inner self or of cultural sensibilities than needs to be the case if a faith is to maintain its deepest insights.

We recall that the Gospels might never have been written, and that only the 'doctrine' mode of Christian statement, initiated, in his own particular epistolary medium, by Paul, would have been available from early Christianity. And, as we saw, as far as their second-century acceptance was concerned, that early excursion into 'story' mode as a way of writing out faith was soon nullified by a failure to keep hold of their original theological message or indeed their mode of working. It was assumed that they were in effect assimilable into a single unity, and treated as an apostolic presence rather than, for example, a collection of theological and ethical statements. Recall that the last persons that we know of to have understood Mark's intended message were Matthew and Luke, who wrote to counter and supplant him. They wrote to this end chiefly because they disagreed with his theology, but they did maintain his mode of 'story'. It may be that they wrote thus not so much because they had stores of Jesus' words that must not be lost, but because they (each) had a different vision of Christian belief and life which they were keen to propagate, with the authority of the memory of Jesus. We can be pretty sure, however, that the canonizing of the four was done without an appreciation of the real character of their diversity. It was to do with bringing into unity the products of different supposed apostolic traditions, with 'Matthew' and 'John' standing in their own right, and with Mark seen as representing Peter and Luke as the locum for Paul. We can imagine that it would have taken many hours of conference to persuade any of these authors to share covers with the others for the rest of time, perhaps all the more so as the distinctive force of their various outlooks was no longer felt – an intolerable fate for any author.

It has taken recent study to make it possible (and via the lectionaries relatively easy, especially if the preacher helps) for people at last to hear the distinctive voices and enter into the

four 'visions' of Christian faith. For those accustomed to the
'doctrine' mode of Christian communication, it can be a
bewildering or destabilizing experience. And of course it may
raise the question: which mode is to prevail? They are not easy
bedfellows. The 'story' mode has the incalculable Christian
advantage that, from the start, it faces us with Jesus – not as a
doctrinal figure (as, for example, in the Nicene Creed or traditional
schemes of Christian doctrine), but as one who taught and acted
on behalf of God, and made a number of distinctive impressions
which we can receive (though admittedly it may be hard to
penetrate far behind them – if one were to wish to do it). At the
simplest, he was a Jesus about whom much was written concerning
the period between his coming and his death, which remained a
blank as far as those working in the 'doctrine' mode were
concerned! What we believe about him and how we respond to
him should surely be conditioned by that material, even though
it comes to us filtered through the styles of belief held by the
evangelists. What is fundamentally important for the mode of
'story' is to establish that Jesus was indeed a figure about whom
such accounts could be formed and written.

An understanding and acceptance of the Gospels in their
diversity prepares us for a feature of statement in the 'doctrine'
mode that has often proved a stumbling-block and an
embarrassment: the fact of (often tortuous) development in
Christian understanding and statement. The more authoritatively
doctrinal formulations have been sponsored by church bodies,
the more reluctant the sponsors have generally been to understand
or accept (let alone welcome) development. Commenting on
the lines by W. H. Auden that stand at the head of this chapter,
J. C. Oates, writing in the *Times Literary Supplement* for 25
May 2001, wrote: 'The metaphor is a striking one, and if we
pursue it, disturbing.' Words are seen as inevitably 'to be con-
sumed, digested, "modified" and, presumably, excreted'. When
it comes to venerable words of faith, this has always proved a
difficult lesson to accept. At best, it has been a matter of building
on what exists, never replacing or pulling down – unless there is
to be a major upheaval such as the Reformation. Yet the Gospels
show to us maturity in difference, presented before our eyes. Or
rather the possibility of maturity being evoked in us; for it cannot

be that the evangelists themselves rejoiced in their diversity, or indeed knew of different responses to Jesus, side by side, as we can now identify and appreciate them, with their contradictions and inconsistencies of theological stance. They are, all the same, an encouragement for mature and comprehending difference. They may also encourage the possibility of rejection: to consider Mark alongside Matthew is, as we saw, to ask whether, on certain basic subjects and with regard to certain basic stances, the two can both be equally valid in their responses to Jesus. There may be choices to be made. In this way, the Gospels not only inform and edify, but also challenge us to decide where we stand on the modern versions of issues that already faced Christian communities in the last decades of the first century.

In this perspective, 'development' should not always be seen as building layer upon layer of a secure edifice, but as also including demolition in order to build again. One can only be amazed at the extraordinarily heavy weather church authorities have tended to make of changes which new circumstances may demand, and at their reluctance to adopt new ways of 'following' Jesus or expressing faith. At the same time of course, equally significant developments, perhaps of a much more dubious or far-reaching character, take place and cause little more than a ripple. Hard to persuade church bodies to consider how God is now to be spoken of, or where the legacy of Jesus may now be truly used; easy to get them to discuss matters concerning arrangements for the corps of the Church's ministers; hard to get them to be continually appalled by failures to act on so many main features of Jesus' picture of our place in the world and the priorities of our duties to one another; relatively easy to secure prohibitions of the minutiae of sexual behaviour. Examples of the two categories spring easily to mind. What matters here is the character of the picture which the Gospels, as now understood, present to us – once they are valued as primary expressions of faith.

Mostly, of course, they have been secondary to statements in the 'doctrine' mode. They may contribute an occasional phrase to a creed: 'whose kingdom shall have no end', for instance, in the Nicene Creed, quotes Luke 1.33, at the expense of the contrary doctrine found in 1 Corinthians 15.28. Conclusions arrived at by way of the 'doctrine' mode found the latter to be false. In cases such as this, it was the doctrine that determined the use made of scriptural texts as much as the reverse. We may now feel that to make a definition on a matter of this kind (supposing it was sensible at all), whether by using the quasi-poetic vision of Paul or that of Luke, was a muddling thing to do, an inappropriate use of ideas from one cultural context to determine concepts arrived at in another.

Sometimes doctrines are in effect discarded. It rarely happens formally. The Reformation was the great convulsion in the Western Church's history when there was large-scale formal jettisoning of old and official beliefs (including, as we saw, prayers for the dead, a huge cultural as well as theological shift). More recently, it tends to happen by a process of atrophy. That is, as a result of almost indefinable cultural changes, certain traditional beliefs become literally unbelievable as far as very many are concerned, and, apart from pockets of increasingly eccentric traditionalists, are quietly dropped from the regular agenda. It is not so much that new formal arguments have arisen, been considered, and have prevailed. Rather that a new climate has gradually made these beliefs fade, like it or not. Belief in hell and final judgement, certainly with anything like their old vigour and vividness, are examples; so, more recently, it may be, is life after death. Surveys now reveal not inconsiderable numbers of churchgoers who do not believe in God. In terms of this book's central interest, it may be that the story of Jesus will continue to fascinate and attract allegiance when virtually the whole of the structure of belief that traditionally surrounded him has been abandoned. In cases like the example just given, that would be an extreme development, but it is worth considering how it would stand in principle.

There is a sense, it seems, that development of this kind is beyond any authority's power to control. There can be sanctions and formal documents, but in the Church at large these are in vain; and even those issuing the sanctions and the documents may be doing it out of a sense of duty rather than with any hope of making the traditional teaching live as it once lived, that is, in people's (including their own) hearts and souls. The experience of hearing a preacher threatening hell to an audience whom he had first attracted by telling jokes showed that, being a not insensitive or heartless man, he cannot have truly believed his own preaching. It would be impossible to joke with those for whom you foresaw such a fate. It was not, one suspects, part of Savonarola's homiletic style.

From this point of view, the 'story' mode is itself beyond controlling. But there is also the suggestion that, in a certain way, it is bound to outrun the 'doctrine' mode. Recent, highly sophisticated formulations of traditional doctrine in a systematic way (far removed from any sense of 'story' mode that finds its model and source in the Gospels) win small numbers to welcome them or find them intelligible. This may be of course no reflection at all on the intrinsic value or fidelity of such endeavours; merely a comment on a failure in the intellectual possibilities in a secularized culture where theological discrimination has all but disappeared.

The virtues of the 'story' mode may be internal to itself and independent of potential popularity at any particular time. They do seem to include, as the Gospels illustrate, as far back as Christian faith can take us, an acceptance of diversity and response to circumstance. The Gospels' ways of framing their narratives depended on the minds of their authors as they considered the needs of their audiences, with narrative as their manner of proceeding: let them hear this perception of Jesus and be moved to receive and then develop their own perception in the setting of life. And there is a sense, both then and now, in which their manner of expression does have affinities with the surrounding culture, creating bridges of intelligibility, when doctrinal schemes do not. The Gospels were not wholly unlike other books about figures in the ancient world; and the story of Jesus continues to stimulate modern imaginative yet sensitive responses in painting, sculpture, film and literature. 'Story' is a manner of almost infinite fluidity, yet in this case as in others (e.g. the Homeric epics), it is not unmoored to its beginnings. It has a large measure of that currently valued quality, 'respect', both for those who first wrote and for those who then receive and carry forward. Of course the original propagators would probably be dissatisfied with the ways they have been received, and there is a duty of respect also toward those givers of the story, so that movement and development are not simply haphazard. Yet there is no eliminating of subjectivity with its risk of strangeness: we know how apocryphal embellishments of, for example, the infancy stories of the Gospels became standard parts of the repertoire of medieval Christianity at popular (and artistic) level. It is beyond anyone's power to define what one day may seem 'acceptable'. As we have seen, the 'doctrine' mode offers no sure relief, for it too moves unpredictably, despite claims to the contrary and despite accommodations (fudges?) that strive to make continuities out of palpable novelties (see 'Infallibility and Historical Revelation', in Farrer, 1976).

Yet, however strange later generations may feel the developments of the story to be and however much they may demand the apparent 'control' which the 'doctrine' mode seems to contribute (while taking its own equally strange theoretical turns), the optimistic response is to say that the later manifestations are in some way unfoldings of the old theme, the blossoming of an identifiable original plant. Always they are variations on the old theme, necessarily, in conservatives as well as recognized innovators, taking new forms, as new circumstances arise. The advantage of 'story' is that it gives room for the teller to 'breathe' and yet to hold in mind and spirit the haunting original in Jesus, as he was responded to at the start; this, rather than the Jesus of formal abstractions and allegedly fixed beliefs that, for all their possible theoretical value, remove him from the life of flesh and blood. Once more: the creed says nothing and the leading doctrinal formulations say nothing about him, in relation to the human scene, between arriving and departing. It is, to say the least, a weakness, especially in relation to one of whom 'incarnation' (he 'dwelt among us') is the major feature.

Whether believers or not, many people who observe the degree of development, diversity and even backtracking in the forms and content of Christian expression, feel a sense of impropriety, even vertigo. What sense can we give to such a range of phenomena, apparently disorderly and unpredictable at so many points? No good appealing to Scripture, because patently Scripture has either been defied or been used and interpreted in so many different ways as to offer no firm criterion. No good appealing to church authority, because, despite forms of words and patterns of teaching, people insist on going their own way, impelled by the spirit of the age, and the church authority itself fails to move in a straight line of logically developing provision.

The musical image of theme and variations offers as good an analogy as any for trying to see order in the apparent chaos. In the case of the musical form, each variation has its own validity, provided that it is recognizably (though perhaps only with difficulty) related to the theme: that is, there must be a kind of integrity in the relationship. And there may of course be dispute about it; and the need for the exercise of judgement brings obvious echoes of the situation in our case. Yet judges may err, or rather, the judging is less a deciding than a discriminating, and there can be legitimate discussion about the grounds for it. The mere issue of a fiat is not helpful, nor does it carry conviction in the case of a variation's appropriateness or legitimacy. Moreover, variations may be endless in their variety, provided the human spirit is sufficiently creative. The process is without end. As in our own case, surrounding cultural ethos will determine the kinds of variations that are composed and found acceptable. Over time, such variations may even, musically, be incompatible, incongruous, in relation to each other; nevertheless, they may stand, because they have legitimacy, each in its own context.

In this way, we can see a way of accommodating even evident contradiction: a church may be antisemitic for centuries, then move fervently in the opposite sense – and the formal contradiction can be comprehended in there being a context in each case which, if not in both cases pleasing or commendable, is at least compre-hensible or explicable; a church may oppose human rights for centuries, and then (in an apparent volte-face) be their fervent advocate, and again contexts can make some (not always total) sense of the contradiction. At the same time, to revert to the musical analogy, one may not find every variation having equal beauty or musical 'honesty'.

So variations on a theme can be without end. They can stretch away into the unknown future of musical development, and there is no reason to call for closure or to feel worried that there is a history still to be made. There can be no sense, then, in attempting to draw lines under the achievement so far, at any particular stage. One may have preferences, even dig one's heels in, but they can be no more than preferences; though some, it is true, will be grounded on more 'informed' judgement. So it is with an old tune which many composers have made attempts to develop in their own idiom.

The diversity in the Gospels offers itself for judgement along these lines. It may apply, for example, to first-century Christian judgements about divorce. Paul quotes Jesus as against it (1 Cor. 7.10–15), but then offers a ground for exception in cases of marriages between believers and unbelievers (a type of case on which, we suppose, Jesus had no occasion to pronounce but which the mission to gentiles had brought to prominence). Mark also quotes Jesus as against it (10.1–12) but in a theological rather than a legalistic spirit; that is, the kingdom will be as Eden restored, and divorce has no place. Matthew (5.32; 19.1–10) has Jesus permit divorce in certain cases, but is acting in a legislating way, presumably out of practical need.

It is a case of variations on a theme: and we too are to 'compose' with all the integrity and moral beauty that we can manage. The same model can be applied to all kinds of topics; for instance, the propriety of infant baptism, where changing social circumstances rather than mere precedent, or even Scripture, notoriously unsure, may be our guide, as we 'compose' suitable variations for our time and place. It will be the same even with regard to fundamental doctrinal tenets; for none is other than the product of a particular time and place. That is to say, none is time-less or place-less. New variations may properly arise, even on such fundamental matters as the person of Jesus, and (it is hard to deny) the existence of God. Though to deny the latter may seem akin to the composing of cacophony that sends most of (but not all of) the audience scurrying for the door.

There is a difficulty concerning the theme on which our endless Christians variations depend. It may be that the analogy is with Edward Elgar's *Enigma Variations*, where there is a distinct relationship between the variations – they recognizably belong together – but no theme is stated – it is left a mystery. It can be guessed but it cannot be known for sure. Jesus left neither writings nor (perforce) tapes or videos of himself (and if he had, would they have eased the difficulty or simply created different conditions for essentially the same situation?). In their absence, the Gospels must stand as among our earliest variations. They have the privilege of proximity to the 'theme', and create a certain kind of norm for the variations that follow; nevertheless, any capacity they may be supposed to have to bind or dictate is limited by their status as no more than variations. So from one point of view they are privileged (as close to the theme in its statement, the new injection of the life of Jesus); from another, they are not privileged at all – that is, if the music is to live and be itself a means to life, the variations must continue to be made.

As we saw in the earlier chapters of this book, the Gospels are not chronicles – they are far more creative than that; so they are not in the least (in our present terms) musical plod, but already enterprising instances of a process that has seen a multitude of examples of the same. Always, for many, this will create timidity, even panic. How can we trust this variation or that to have integrity? But then the question that follows is: how can we bear to accept the circumstances of our lives, ever conditioned by time and place, from which no Church can free us? In terms of our metaphor, perhaps the chief move is to welcome the necessary fact that the variations proliferate, while the theme itself eludes us, almost heard but never trapped. Was not this the key to the variations having their perilous though inevitable freedom?

Whatever the strength of the arguments for a 'theme-and-variations' model, cohering so well with both historical observation and the 'story' mode of the statement of faith, there is little hope of its ever making headway in the more formal workings of church life. Liberal Catholic Anglicanism, more a 'tendency' than even a movement, has perhaps the best chance of expressing it: it has the possibility of combining strength of Christian eucharistic community, a sense of continuity with Christian history, and an openness to the inevitability of even radical development in belief and practice. In other words, it ought to be able to accept variation upon variation, in unforeseen and provisional ways, and to entertain an alert contentment with some untidiness of mind! There is little to be hoped from the 'great churches', whether Roman Catholic, Orthodox or Protestant: they will always put their weight behind the priority of the 'doctrine' mode, with its tendency to a belief in inflexibility even when history proves the human inability to stick to it (and, as recent decades have shown, with special rigidity in relation to matters concerning clerical order). It is an irony of history that the Christian movements most universalistic in their theological, moral and social aspirations, simple, pure and unifying (they hoped) in doctrinal priorities, were those constantly fragmenting movements of the radical Reformation in 1520s Germany and 1640s England (see Williams, 1962; Scott, 2000, chs 11–12). They combined an acceptance of movement with a sense of 'essentials', but lacked any realistic sense of history or indeed of the humanly possible, for all their glorious vigour. And, while *acting* in the mode of 'story', it was not their way, any more than anyone else's, of 'reading' Christian origins.

It seems clear that the 'story' mode, so long underprivileged by comparison with the 'doctrine' mode of Christian expression, has every reason to assert its right for at the very least equal treatment, a full hearing. Traditionally, it has been regarded as at best ancillary, perhaps even 'folksy', showing itself in nativity plays and church windows and, more profoundly, in imaginative private meditation; while reputable and reliable Christian statement, alone to be preferred and normative, has always felt itself to be (and been largely seen as being) dependable and reputable, even though it has found itself claiming continuities where they do not exist or tolerating changes while at the same time denying their theoretical possibility.

Though he is less concerned with the historical dimension which has often been the case in this discussion, Wesley A. Kort has made the essential point in the medium of prose: 'Thoughts and events, beliefs and facts, we tend to assume, antedate narrative and text. We are fascinated by and seek to establish our identity on a non-narrative, non-textual reality, and we consider narrative texts to be prisons where facts and ideas are kept and from which they must be freed' (see the head of this chapter).

A similarly key statement appears in verse in William Plomer's poem , 'A Church in Bavaria' (1973, pp. 256ff.). (For a full discussion of the poem, see Houlden, 1986, ch. 11.) Here it suffices to quote the final verse which grasps the nettle of the absent theme, of which only the variations are available for us, both to absorb and to create; so long as we do it with integrity and discrimination towards even our most outrageous fellow variation-makers of past and present! He traces the absence of the theme to the key fact that Jesus 'never wrote a word'. Instead he threw his words away, so leaving others to make what they could of them. In Christian terms, this fact implies a divine trust in human reactions: words went into the air, awaiting people to hear, retain and consider, in ways that were of course varied from the start. The theme, we may say, vanished into people's memories and into lives lived in the light of them. In this way, Jesus' 'throwing away' of his words ('story') is comparable to his 'throwing away' of his life on the cross ('doctrine?') – and the passion narrative in the Gospels is a meeting place of the two 'modes'. Plomer faces the fact that different models of theology and religion imply different 'worlds' of sensibility – and so, necessarily, of faith.

> Everything bends
>   to re-enact
>   the poem lived,
>   lived, not written,
>   the poem spoken
>   by Christ, who never
> wrote a word
>   saboteur
>   of received ideas
>   who rebuilt Rome
>   with the words he
>   never wrote;
>   whether sacred,
>   whether human,
> himself a sunrise
>   of love enlarged,
>   of love, enlarged.

R. S. Thomas made a similar point, but less provocatively, in 'The Kingdom' (1993, p. 233).

> It's a long way off but inside it
> There are quite different things going on:
> Festivals at which the poor man
> Is king and the consumptive is

Healed: mirrors in which the blind look
At themselves and love looks at them
Back: and industry is for mending
The bent bones and the minds fractured
By life. It's a long way off, but to get
There takes no time and admission
Is free, if you will purge yourself
Of desire, and present yourself with
Your need only and the simple offering
Of your faith, green as a leaf.

It is frequently said that Christianity stands alongside Judaism and Islam as one of the religions of 'the book'. This is of course correct in the superficial sense that all use Scriptures and share some of them. But Christianity is not a religion of the book in the sense that Scripture is primary. We read it, go on thinking about it, preach from it, meditate on it, quote it, even swear by it when it is thought our word should be believed. But it is not fundamental. Even those Christians who revere it greatly show that they recognize this by trusting so readily in new translations – all translations being by their nature faulty; not to speak of the fact that all translation is interpretation. Jews and Muslims distrust translations for these excellent reasons. I recall a bar mitzvah when the proceedings were halted because there was an uncertainty in a letter in the scroll that was being chanted. Elders gathered and held, in effect, a seminar lasting perhaps 20 minutes to settle the point. Such an event would be unthinkable in even the most Scripture-loving Christian gathering. In that sense, we are, when it comes to difficulties, often cavalier about the Bible. And the constant demand for modern, allegedly more intelligible translations indicates that evangelism has higher priority than scriptural accuracy. We prefer to let Jesus be available through Scripture to the letter of Scripture itself: it is the 'sunrise of love enlarged' which attracts and holds us, however obliquely.

For that matter, we now realize that scriptural accuracy is itself a chimera. The manuscript tradition has many uncertainties, and the quest for 'the original' of, for instance, the Gospel of Mark may well be hopeless from the start, for why should not

Mark himself have produced a number of copies, each different in some respects (see Parker, 1997)?

In this perspective and in terms of our image, Scripture itself is among the variations on the theme that lies behind them, both as a whole and in its parts. When placed in the Christian canon, the Old Testament writings are themselves among the variations, as they are read, in numerous ways, in a Christian context: they are, we may say, prospective, just as the Gospels are retrospective variations. That task has become much more difficult and much more hazy in the light of the development of historically oriented 'Old Testament studies' or, more candidly, 'Hebrew Bible studies'; but in principle that is how the continuing presence of these writings in Christian use must be somehow understood, rather than as contributions to historical studies or inter-faith relations, both admirable but not necessarily to the point in the context. The question then is whether large tracts of the Old Testament can possibly stand such an understanding. Yet churches show little readiness to put even tentative toes on to the path they were scared from by Marcion in the second century: to mix the metaphors, nettles left ungrasped come home to roost! For Christians, faith centres on Jesus as the decisive agent of God, and all else is witness or response.

This book has been written in the idioms of both New Testament studies and interpretative reflection from a doctrinal perspective, though always hovering, tangibly, have been the present demands of faith. Austin Farrer, who, in a different time and idiom, shared some of these preoccupations, wrote words that help to sum up what has been at stake: 'We identify ourselves with what we adore; the heart that can love Christ is in Christ's keeping' (1970, p. 169). The theme is the one thing needful. That we must for ever seek and listen is the nature of God's invitation to us; and the 'story' awaits us.

Bibliography

Alexander, L., *The Preface to Luke's Gospel.* Cambridge University Press 1993.

Ashton, J., ed., *The Interpretation of John.* SPCK, London, 1986.

Ashton, J., *Understanding the Fourth Gospel.* Clarendon Press, Oxford, 1991.

Auden, W. H., *Collected Poems.* Faber and Faber, London, 1976.

Beavis, M., *Mark's Audience.* Sheffield Academic Press 1989.

Borgen, P., *'God's Agent in the Fourth Gospel'* in Ashton, 1986.

Brown, R. E., *The Community of the Beloved Disciple.* Geoffrey Chapman, Dublin, 1979.

Bultmann, R., *History of the Synoptic Tradition.* 1921, ET Blackwell, Oxford, 1963.

Burridge, R. A., *What Are the Gospels?* Cambridge University Press 1992.

Burridge, R. A., *Four Gospels, One Jesus?* SPCK, London, 1994.

Cahill, M., ed., *The First Commentary on Mark.* Oxford University Press 1998.

Caird, G. B., *New Testament Theology,* ed. L. D. Hurst. Clarendon Press, Oxford, 1994.

Catchpole, D., *Resurrection People.* Darton, Longman & Todd, London, 2000.

Conzelmann, H., *The Theology of Luke.* Faber and Faber, London, 1960.

Drury, J., *Tradition and Design in Luke's Gospel.* Darton, Longman & Todd, London, 1976.

Duffy, E., *The Stripping of the Altars.* Yale University Press, New Haven CT and London, 1992.

Edwards, D. L., *John Donne.* Continuum, London and New York, 2001.

Farrer, A. M., *A Study in St Mark.* Dacre Press, London, 1951.

Farrer, A. M., *A Celebration of Faith,* ed. J. L. Houlden. Hodder & Stoughton, London, 1970.

Farrer, A. M., *Interpretation and Belief,* ed. C. Conti. SPCK, London, 1976.

Fenton, J. C., *More About Mark.* SPCK, London, 2001.

Good, D. J., *Jesus the Meek King.* Trinity Press International, Harrisburg PA, 1999.

Goulder, M. D., *Midrash and Lection in Matthew.* SPCK, London, 1974.

Goulder, M. D., *Luke: A New Paradigm.* Sheffield Academic Press 1989.

Hengel, M., *The Johannine Question.* SCM Press, London, 1989.

Hengel, M., *The Four Gospels and the One Gospel of Jesus Christ.* SCM-Canterbury Press, London, 2000.

Hooker, M. D., *The Message of Mark.* Epworth Press, London, 1983.

Houlden, J. L., *Connections.* SCM Press, London, 1986.

Houlden, J. L., *Backward into Light.* SCM Press, London, 1987.

Houlden, J. L., *Ethics and the New Testament.* T. & T. Clark, Edinburgh, 1992.

Hurtado, L. W., *One God, One Lord.* T. & T. Clark, Edinburgh, second edition 1998.

Käsemann, E., *The Testament of Jesus.* SCM Press, London, 1971.

Klassen, W., *Judas.* SCM Press, London, 1996.

Kort, W. A., *Story, Text and Scripture.* The Pennsylvania State University Press, University Park and London, 1988.

Lightfoot, R. H., *The Gospel Message of St Mark.* Clarendon Press, Oxford, 1950.

Lindars, B., *Behind the Fourth Gospel.* SPCK, London, 1971.

Louth, A., ed., *Early Christian Writings.* Penguin Books, Harmondsworth, 1987.

MacDonald, D. R., *The Homeric Epic and the Gospel of Mark.* Yale University Press, New Haven CT, 2000.

Macquarrie, J., *Principles of Christian Theology.* SCM Press, London, 1966.

Marxsen, W., *Mark the Evangelist.* Abingdon Press, Nashville TN, 1961.

McManners, J., *Death and the Enlightenment*. Clarendon Press, Oxford, 1981.

Muir, E., *Collected Poems*. Faber & Faber, London, 1960.

Norman, E., *Anglican Catechism*. Continuum, London and New York, 2001.

Parker, D. C., *The Living Text of the Gospels*. Cambridge University Press 1997.

Plomer, W., *Collected Poems*. Jonathan Cape, London, 1973.

Rhoads, D. and Michie, D., *Mark as Story*. Fortress Press, Philadelphia PA, 1984.

Rhoads, D., Dewey, A. and Michie, D., *Mark as Story*, revised edition. Fortress Press, Minneapolis MN, 1999.

Richardson C. C., ed., *Early Christian Fathers*, Library of Christian Classics I. SCM Press, London, 1953.

Scott, J., *England's Troubles*. Cambridge University Press 2000.

Stanton, G. N., *A Gospel for a New People*. T. & T. Clark, Edinburgh, 1992.

Thomas, R. S., *Collected Poems*. Phoenix Grant, London, 1993.

Trobisch, D., *The First Edition of the New Testament*. Oxford University Press 2000.

Vanstone, W. H., *The Stature of Waiting*. Darton, Longman & Todd, London, 1982.

Wilken, R. L., *The Myth of Christian Beginnings*. SCM Press, London, 1971.

Williams, G. H., *The Radical Reformation*. Weidenfeld & Nicolson 1962.

Index of Names

Index of Biblical References